Marilyn

FOREVER

By the same author:

Holy Cow!
Celebrity Feuds!
Hollywood Lesbians
Hollywood Gays
Broadway Babylon
An Actor Succeeds
492 Great Things about Being Italian

Marilyn
FOREVER

Musings on an American Icon by the Stars of Yesterday and Today

BOZE HADLEIGH

TAYLOR | TRADE
PUBLISHING

Lanham • Boulder • New York • London

To Ronnie
and the Marilyn fans who
look behind the surface

An imprint of Rowman & Littlefield

Distributed by NATIONAL BOOK NETWORK

Copyright © 2016 by Boze Hadleigh

British Library Cataloguing in Publication Information Available

Library of Congress Cataloging-in-Publication Data

ISBN 978-1-63076-263-6
ISBN 978-1-63076-264-3 (e-book)

∞™ The paper used in this publication meets the minimum requirements of American National Standard for Information Sciences—Permanence of Paper for Printed Library Materials, ANSI/NISO Z39.48-1992.

CONTENTS

Many people don't know that in her own time Marilyn Monroe was often a figure of controversy. For each fan, there was a detractor—among the public and among her peers. To some she was a joke, to others a scandal. Her talent was derided and many critics persistently, and ironically, called her a flash in the pan.

Marilyn rose to fame on her blonde beauty and her body. She survived the scandalous nude photos she'd posed for pre-stardom (they later launched the Playboy empire) and eschewed further nudity until the end of her career. Her ongoing sex appeal limited her professionally and ultimately attracted dangerous attention.

There were other sex symbols during Marilyn's era, but she outshone them all, for she had more than looks. Marilyn had class. More refined and touching than most sexual icons, she was also the girl next door, only lovelier. Her legend grew via revelations of her involvement with the Kennedys.

In death, Marilyn achieved her apotheosis, becoming the most famous female face of the twentieth century. The criticism faded and she became mythologized. Her talent and persona were reassessed. Was she murdered? Suicide or an accidental overdose? Regardless, she lives and shines on, no longer just a star, but a goddess.

CHAPTER 1

Victim

"Kissing her was like kissing Hitler."　　　　　—Tony Curtis, costar, *Some Like It Hot*

"Marilyn Monroe was fabulous, but in my opinion she was too fat."
　　　　　　　　　　—Elizabeth Hurley, model turned actress

"She has breasts of granite and a mind like a gruyère cheese."
—Billy Wilder, MM's two-time director
(*Some Like It Hot* and *The Seven Year Itch*)

"Sadists desire her and masochists adore her."　　　　　—Gene Simmons of KISS

"People are still asking, 'But can she act?' Not that it really matters." —Robert Downey Jr.

"That broad's got a great future behind her."　　　—Constance Bennett, once Hollywood's
top-paid actress, after getting a front and a rear view of Marilyn

"Marilyn Monroe was only smart for ten minutes in her entire life. And that was the time it took her to sign with Twentieth Century Fox."

—Anne Baxter, fellow Fox contract actor (both appeared in *All About Eve*)

"I guess the classic apocryphal Hollywood story is that Marilyn wrote a letter to Albert Einstein. She admired him very much and wanted to have a child by him. So she writes and says, 'Dear Dr. Einstein, If we had a child together, it would be perfection. Because it would have my looks and your brains.'

"So he writes back, 'My dear Miss Monroe, You have to consider the possibility that if we had a child together, it might inherit my looks and your brains.'"

—Shelley Winters, actress and one-time roommate

"I was telling an anecdote to my friend and protégé Marilyn Monroe the other day. I added, 'Of course you realize this story is apocryphal,' and Marilyn said, 'You mean you don't know how to punctuate it?'"
—Sidney Skolsky, columnist, one of several men who claimed to have discovered MM

"Suzanne Somers of *Three's Company*, which she's now departing, is the latest in a long line of dumb blondes beginning with Marilyn Monroe who suddenly strike it surprisingly big. . . . Nor does Somers have a fraction of Marilyn's charisma."

—Paul Rosenfield, columnist, *Los Angeles Times*

"They were always and always calling her a dumb blonde. I'd say the correct word for what she enacted all too often and too well was naive."   —Warren Fisher, publicist and friend

"What passes for feminine appeal these days is rather blatant for my taste. . . . Miss Monroe leaves little to a male's imagination. Marlene Dietrich was more my idea of a beautiful and appealing woman."   —Ronald Colman, movie star

"I have just come from the Actors Studio, where I saw Marilyn Monroe. She had no girdle on, her ass was hanging out. She is a disgrace to the industry."
—Joan Crawford

"I'm not asking to be catty, but if Marilyn hadn't married Joe DiMaggio, who was a bigger icon than she was at first, how really famous would she have become? Sometimes matrimony means more to an actress's career than her movies. . . . I mean, look at Elizabeth Taylor."   —Joan Rivers

"I was in Arthur Miller's [play] *After the Fall*. I did not play the Marilyn character. . . . I could sympathize with Marilyn, but I didn't want to be like her. I wanted to make the rules of my own life."   —Faye Dunaway

"The girl's got something, but I don't think she can sing."
—Darryl F. Zanuck, Fox studio chief who believed MM was dubbed when he heard her on the *Gentlemen Prefer Blondes* musical soundtrack

"She didn't believe in herself. What she saw in the mirror wasn't enough for her. It was enough for everybody else, but not for her. She hardly knew the meaning of the word 'confidence.'"   —Jane Russell, costar, *Gentlemen Prefer Blondes*

"Sometimes we ran to over thirty takes until Marilyn finally got it right. That meant I had to be as good on take twenty-five or thirty as on the first and second takes, in case that was the one they printed. . . . But I couldn't be angry with Marilyn. She didn't do it on purpose. She had no bitchery in her."
—Lauren Bacall, costar, *How to Marry a Millionaire*

"They keep comparing me to her, but why? Because we are both blonde? If I am a sex symbol, she is not. Her movies are very innocent, and she is never without her clothes. To a Frenchman, she is not a sex symbol. We know about sex in this country!"
—Brigitte Bardot, French actress and rival bombshell

"I think she was funny, like in comedies, but she was overrated. I think anyone who keeps being famous after they're dead is overrated."   —fellow "Marilyn" Marilyn Manson

"She was very good, portraying Miss Caswell, an actress who can't act. Miss Monroe was a clever comedienne . . . . On the set [of *All About Eve*] she didn't stand out in any way. She just did her job, seemed sweet, and left. Nobody guessed what she would become. I think she was more impressive on camera than in person."   —Bette Davis

"I got fed up with Twentieth Century Fox and Hollywood when Marilyn Monroe came on the scene and they actually built her up into this giant of tiny proportions. The things they let her get away with! On account of the money she made for them.

"For instance, she took direction not from her directors but her lesbian drama coach, whom they all said she was sleeping with. That's not my concern, but it got my goat when they took a no-talent and began ignoring those of us who could actually act!" —Anne Baxter

4

"That dyke!"   —Elizabeth Taylor, referring to Marilyn, as quoted in Norman Mailer's
book *Marilyn* (Taylor threatened to sue Mailer, but he had evidence of the utterance;
MM may have been occasionally bisexual.)

"She killed Clark Gable, you know. She'd grown up idolizing him, and when they finally
got to work together, he was an old man with a heart condition and she was always late at
the Nevada location, so he had to wait in the broiling sun for her to show up."
     —DeWitt Bodeen, screenwriter (Gable, who died at sixty, insisted on doing
his own strenuous stunts for 1961's *The Misfits*.)

"What is this thing that blondes get from the press? Special immunity by way of hair color?
Look at Grace Kelly. . . . We all knew that Aristotle Onassis, who owned the Monte Carlo
Casino, ordered Prince Rainier to marry a Hollywood blonde for the publicity and tourism.
     "It was rumored that Rainier almost chose Marilyn Monroe. If he had, no doubt she
too would have been immortalized as virginal, talented, and a non-addict. . . . At least
Marilyn wasn't a hypocrite. Unlike Grace, she didn't pretend to be a sanctimonious
virgin."
     —Anne Baxter

"She was lovable on the screen, yes. In real life, she was so concerned with herself, she
was just insensitive."   —Estelle Winwood, actress who appeared in MM's last
completed film, *The Misfits*, and lived to the age of 101

"Marilyn was so overly sensitive, if she got really upset, she would
start to menstruate, and I do not exaggerate."
—Robert Mitchum, costar, *River of No Return*

"You know what her biggest problem was? She couldn't, or wouldn't, stand up for herself. . . . I saw Mitchum treat her lousy a couple of times, and she just took it. The first time she smiled, like she was hoping he'd quit carrying on. The other time, she cowered, like a little girl about to cry. . . . The way he treated her was shabby. The way she let him was disappointing. Most gals in this business have a much tougher hide than that."

—Rory Calhoun, costar, *River of No Return*

"Marilyn reached a point where she was sick and tired of men. They all wanted to use her, in one way or another. As she got older, she didn't trust most other actresses. The only people she felt comfortable or safe with were kids. She loved children, treated them like little treasures. It was touching and sad."   —Susan Strasberg, actress, friend, and daughter of MM's acting coach Lee Strasberg

"Of course I think I'm smarter than Marilyn! . . . I'm still here, aren't I?"
—Madonna, speaking in her fifties (Her early music video for "Material Girl" was a takeoff of MM's "Diamonds Are a Girl's Best Friend" number in *Gentlemen Prefer Blondes*.)

"One of the things that's tragic about Marilyn Monroe is that her beginning was so sad, and her ending was so sad. She wasn't a star for very long, and the early years and the last years were so unhappy. You have to wonder, were those few years worth all the pain?"

—Jamie Lee Curtis

"I don't like to think about her, because she makes you want to cry." —Michael Jackson

"Marilyn was no dumb bunny. She knew how to gain sympathy. . . . When she spoke about her past, she exaggerated it. She made it sound worse than it was. She became the poor little orphan girl that nobody wanted, bounced from home to home. It made her more pitiable, and thus more acceptable to a public that would otherwise think she was too blatantly carnal."
—Sheilah Graham, columnist

"I read a book by Lois Banner about Marilyn, about the eleven different homes she grew up in. It was very illuminating, very sad. . . . You know, Marilyn used to babysit our kids. She loved doing it."
—Eli Wallach, costar, *The Misfits*

"I thought she wasn't much of an actress, until one day I interviewed Miss Monroe about her childhood. I knew her mother had sent her to live with relatives not long after she was born, but my goodness . . . it was like Little Orphan Annie without any of the cheery parts. I nearly cried.
   "She was so composed, so unsolicitous of any sympathy, very matter of fact and forlorn. As if she was holding back the emotion, being brave. I didn't think she was a good actress yet. Not until later, when I found out the picture she painted was quite distorted, for public consumption."
—Dorothy Manners, gossip columnist

"Virtually all the families Norma Jean lived with as a child and teenager were relatives of her mother's. They weren't strangers. They were not ogres."
—Norman Mailer, novelist and MM biographer

"It's often been said that Marilyn may have been molested as a child or girl. In her lifetime, that wasn't something people discussed at any length. It was all too common for a female growing up to be sexually abused by a male in the house, whether a relative or not, and there were actually incest-exception laws on the books that excused such men's behavior from prosecution of any kind. . . . It was a terrible era in which to grow up female, and Marilyn may have carried lifelong scars from it."

—Dr. Betty Berzon, psychologist and author

"Marilyn Monroe routinely told interviewers who asked that her mother was dead. Eventually it was discovered the woman was alive and working at a modest job. By then Marilyn was a big star, and big stars always have their detractors. So she explained that she'd been protecting her mother's privacy, which may be true. What all the media wanted was a photo of Gladys, to compare, to see if Marilyn got her looks from her. . . . Gladys was very private, she shunned the spotlight and was something of a frump."

—Don Murray, costar, *Bus Stop*

"Most women liked Marilyn or sympathized with her. Women stars didn't, necessarily. One who didn't was Liz Taylor. She once called Marilyn a 'dyke,' and Norman Mailer, in that book of his—you know it became a bestseller because it had that gorgeous cover, I think it was a close-up from her final, incomplete movie—he repeated that. Taylor threatened to sue if he didn't remove it, but he had the evidence, so it stayed in the book.

"Obviously Elizabeth Taylor isn't anti-gay. But that's not to say she's pro-lesbian, and I guess she'd heard that Marilyn was maybe bi, that she had a same-sex romance or two along the way."

—Warren Cowan, Hollywood publicist

"Marilyn did try to help her mother, but the woman was very proud. Also prudish. For a brief time, she lived with Marilyn but disapproved of her clothes and roles . . . very critical of her. Jealous, I suppose. She had another daughter, by another man or husband—named Berniece Miracle, believe it or not. She seemed to prefer her over Marilyn. Probably because she was nowhere as successful as Marilyn."

—Arthur Marx, author and son of Groucho

"It seems like everyone who ever knew Marilyn has written a book about her, from her half sister to her first husband to her maid to her shrinks to her friends. If you learn something that's new and true and not overly intrusive about her from the books, fine. People are still curious. But I think most of them did it just for the money, and to me that's victimization."—Alan Hale Jr. (aka the Skipper on *Gilligan's Island*), an early costar

"The prize for chutzpah goes to Tony Curtis. During [the filming of] *Some Like It Hot*, he tells the world kissing her was 'like kissing Hit-luh.' Made it clear he couldn't stand her . . . couldn't stand her being first-billed even though her role was smaller. Decades later, long after she's dead, Curtis writes a 'mem-wah' of the movie and pretends he had an affair with her! I'd hate to have his nerve in my tooth."

—Gerard Tompkins, Australian film historian

"Within ten years of Miss Monroe's death, there was a virtual library of biographies about her. Most of the authors treated her like a freak of nature or a terminal victim. The first really sympathetic, psychologically insightful biography was by a woman, Lena Pepitone, who'd worked for Marilyn. Someone who'd actually listened to her."   —Elsa Lanchester
(aka the Bride of Frankenstein), wife of MM's costar Charles Laughton

"It's some coincidence that the studio system's two final female icons, Marilyn Monroe and Elizabeth Taylor—neither born Jewish—both died Jewish."
—Sherwood Schwartz, creator of *The Brady Bunch*

"Our makeup man on *Little House on the Prairie* was an old pro, Allan 'Whitey' Snyder. One day he showed me a gold money clip he always carried. It was engraved with the words 'While I'm Still Warm—Marilyn.' Whitey had been Marilyn Monroe's makeup man from her first screen test all the way to the day she died.

"What the engraving referred to was this: Marilyn used to laugh and tell Whitey, 'Oh, Whitey, your makeup is so wonderful, when I die I want you to make me up while I'm still warm!' When she died at thirty-six, he went to the funeral home and applied makeup to the face of his now dead friend. The task was extremely traumatic for him and required large amounts of alcohol to complete. I was told Whitey never fully recovered emotionally and that I should be careful when discussing Marilyn in his presence."   —Alison Arngrim (aka Nellie Oleson)

"Bette Davis was under contract to Universal for a year. They dropped her because she didn't have enough sex appeal. She went to Warners, and the rest is history. Likewise, in 1946 a former Goldwyn Girl named Donna Hamilton and her friend, model Norma Jeane Dougherty, were taken to Twentieth Century Fox by a talent scout, and both were signed for a year at $125 a week. They were trained in singing, dancing, and acting.

"But in 1947, the geniuses at Fox decided they couldn't afford to pay both, so they kept the one they thought showed the most promise, and let go the one they'd renamed Marilyn Monroe."   —Maxine Cheshire, columnist

"There was a myth that Norma Jean Baker was named after the movie stars Norma Shearer and Jean Harlow. However, neither was a star when the future Marilyn Monroe was born in 1926."   —Pauline Kael, movie critic (Shearer was in fact starring in movies by then.)

"I've read at least twice that Marilyn's last name was from President [James] Monroe. And that she was named after the movie star Norma Talmadge. Both untrue. . . . Monroe was her mother's maiden name."   —Susan Strasberg, actress and friend

"There were different spellings of Marilyn Monroe's original first names and surnames. When she was born, it wasn't clear who her father was, and her mother's husband had left the mother, so the mother tried to hide that. . . . The mother had been something of a man-chaser when young, then hypocritically turned to religion and was ashamed not of herself or the men in her life, but her daughter."   —Curt Siodmak, screenwriter, *The Wolf Man*

"Norma Jean was pretty, which means little in Tinseltown. Marilyn was beautiful. She made herself so. She may have had her nose slightly thinned, and there was talk of a small chin implant. I heard that she got it after overhearing someone at a party refer to her as a chinless wonder. Of course she also had her hair blondened beyond what it was, and that's where I can claim credit. I eventually gave her the blonde-on-blonde look with which she's now most famously associated."
—George Masters, hairdresser

"When Tina Louise became Ginger on *Gilligan's Island*, she did so after her insistence and our approval that her image and dialogue be changed. Ginger Grant, marooned movie star, was originally written as cynical and rather tough. But after the first Ginger was replaced— as were the first Professor and Mary Ann—Tina said she wanted her character to be a combination of Lucille Ball and Marilyn Monroe—funny but wistful, a gorgeous mantrap yet an innocent victim of circumstance."   —Sherwood Schwartz, TV writer and producer

"I thought Marilyn Monroe should have played Holly Golightly.
She was closer to it than Audrey Hepburn, who I love, but she's
European and elegant. Holly was a hillbilly named Lula Mae passing
as a sophisticate. She was also an expensive but somewhat innocent call
girl. Emotionally, she was very fragile. The tears were very close to the
surface. . . . I'm not sure how Audrey got the part, but the public
liked it. It was a big fat hit, and I couldn't complain about that."
—Truman Capote on the film version of his novella *Breakfast at Tiffany's*

"Marilyn had definitely suffered in her life. I mean, no father, a mother who couldn't keep her for long and who had to be institutionalized, and then the years of struggling from model and pinup girl to starlet and underrated star, with sexploitation and casting couch episodes along the way. So when she knew others were suffering, she had more empathy for them than most movie stars ever do."   —Jack Lemmon, costar, *Some Like It Hot*

"Yes, he did."   —Allan "Whitey" Snyder, MM's makeup man, when asked whether
Joe DiMaggio had struck his wife

"On her honeymoon with Joe DiMaggio in Japan, Marilyn was asked to go to Korea and entertain the troops. She immediately said yes and did several shows, brightening the lives of dozens of thousands of soldiers. She remembered it as one of the happiest times of her life, because they so appreciated her going there. She also said it was one of the saddest times, because so many of the boys were homesick and afraid.

"I know Marilyn kept cards and letters from that trip. . . . It was one topic that could easily bring a tear to her eye. She really felt for those boys, and [she] got hundreds of thank-you letters from their mothers."

—Betty Grable, costar, *How to Marry a Millionaire*

"When Marilyn went to Korea, she didn't go as a movie star—you know, the Bob Hope publicity route. Hope was known, in Korea and Vietnam, to fly off the moment his show was over and the cameras stopped rolling, and he wouldn't venture near the dangerous areas. Unlike Marilyn. She stayed after each and every show to chat with the soldiers, to sign autographs, have pictures taken, plus she went to the front lines, near the combat zones. She could have chosen the easy route, with the big cities and the southern cities, but she didn't. Marilyn was a trooper . . . she had a heart."

—Jerry Orbach, actor, *Law and Order*

"When she married Joe DiMaggio, he was still better known than her. So she got a lot of flak, as if she married for the publicity. But she didn't know a thing about baseball and she barely knew who DiMaggio was when she started dating him."

—Warren Fisher, publicist and friend

"Their courtship and their post-divorce friendship lasted longer than the marriage, which only took up part of 1954. . . . Joe was an old-fashioned Italian American. He expected Marilyn to give up her work and focus on him. He also expected his wife to not flaunt her charms for other men to enjoy."   —Dean Martin (né Dino Crocetti)

"Joe's glory days were mostly behind him. Marilyn's were mostly ahead of her. When they met, their publicity multiplied, because each was a famous public figure. Neither would have gotten as much coverage solo.

"Joe admired Marilyn's figure and liked the flattery and prestige he got from being her beau. She must have realized his reflected fame could only help her career. But how unrealistic was it if he thought she'd throw it all away to go live in San Francisco with a retired man, be a housewife, and make pasta for him and his relatives. What was he thinking?"   —Bobby Darin (né Walden Cassotto), singer and actor

"Well, no man can excel at two national pastimes."
—actor-musician Oscar Levant on DiMaggio divorcing Monroe
(She filed for divorce.)

"There was more than a bit of grumbling when Marilyn paired up with Arthur Miller. Is it not obvious why? She'd finished with DiMaggio, an 'all-American' boy, star athlete, and a Catholic. To take up with Miller, whose name was 'all-American,' but he was a leftie, an intellectual, a writer . . . and a Jew. That was more than enough to cause an angry surge in anti-Marilyn news coverage."   —Eli Wallach, costar, *The Misfits*

"I remember reading some bitchy newspaper columnist who said that as soon as she met Arthur Miller and he looked receptive, Marilyn Monroe reportedly decided to pursue him with an eye to landing a husband who could write wonderful plays and scripts for her. Later, in a book, I read that Marilyn had already met Miller several years before.

"Besides, he never wrote her a play and did only one so-so script for her, *The Misfits*."
—Jan Murray, actor-comedian

"When Marilyn Monroe moved to New York to further study acting, there was criticism and ridicule. When she married the playwright behind *The Crucible* and *Death of a Salesman*, there was that much more criticism and ridicule. Also of him, for allegedly marrying beneath himself and 'selling out' to Hollywood."
—Sir Cecil Beaton, photographer-designer

"It's seldom acknowledged . . . that Marilyn Monroe was brave to date and marry Arthur Miller. He wrote *The Crucible*, ostensibly about the Salem witch hunts, but [it was] a pointed reference to the Republican Congress's political witch hunts [of the 1950s]. Not only was he blacklisted, he was ordered to appear before the House Un-American Activities Committee to answer their inane charges and name names. He did not name names.

"But he did lose friends and associates who feared being associated with him, since the witch hunters also targeted people by association. Marilyn stood by Miller, at a time when most ambitious actresses would have feared secretly dating him, let alone marrying him."
—John Cusack

"I can understand Marilyn's intense desire to be a mother. We each lost our mother[s] at an early age—mine to death and she to a mental asylum. When a female loses her mother prematurely, her emotional foundation is rocked severely. . . . There's a need to be mothered that somehow may express itself as the need to become a mother, to diminish or exchange that loss by trying to give what you no longer have."
—Angelina Jolie

"I remember people openly scoffing at the idea of Marilyn Monroe wanting to be a mother, she was such a sex symbol figure. Much of the news coverage of her [three] miscarriages was very cavalier, very dismissive. They almost blamed her for having gotten pregnant in the first place. That has to be very psychologically revealing about them."
—Rory Calhoun

"It strikes me as misleading and unrealistic to keep emphasizing Marilyn Monroe's sadness over her miscarriages but not her sadness over losing her mother. My guess is that strikes a young woman much harder. You can get pregnant again. You can't have another mother."   —Russell Johnson (aka the Professor on *Gilligan's Island*)

"It's more of a male proposition that a woman feels incomplete without a child. Women are strong. Marilyn was strong. To survive even as long as she did, she had to be strong. We get over shocks, disappointments, abuse. What we don't need is men telling us how sad it all was and is."
—Ruby Dee, actress

"Lots of movie stars, especially actresses, don't have kids. They don't always have the time, especially when they're still attractive and marketable. I saw a documentary where it was like Marilyn Monroe's biggest tragedy in life was that she couldn't have a child. It was mentioned three or four times by this authoritative male voice. I mean, if she'd wanted a child all that much, she could certainly have adopted."

—Lesley Gore, singer-songwriter, "You Don't Own Me"

"There are plenty of women in and out of Hollywood who prefer the label 'child-free' to 'childless.' If a woman really wants a child to take care of, she can adopt or marry."

—Joan Rivers

"The coverage of Marilyn's final months is often still on the order of 'She'd reached the end of her rope.' If you read the facts about 1962, she was on an upswing. Even after the firing by Fox, they were eager and greedy to negotiate with her, and they did. Marilyn was revving up on the publicity and professional fronts, she lost weight, and looked better than she had in years. She'd also recently bought her first home and had plans . . . no way was she in a tailspin. Short of murder, which I very much doubt, she unfortunately suffered an accidental drug overdose.

"People who regularly take drugs think they know exactly how far they can go, but different drugs—and alcohol too is a drug—interact badly, sometimes fatally. Anyone can guess wrong, and alas Marilyn miscalculated."

—A. C. Lyles, Paramount Pictures executive

"I read a book about her where it said Marilyn was terrified of inheriting her mother's mental illness. It also said she wanted to have a baby more than anything in the world. There's a disconnect there: Wouldn't she have been 'terrified' or at least afraid that her baby might inherit mental illness? I don't say this to be contrary, but logical."
—director Robert Mulligan, director, *To Kill a Mockingbird*

"One thing I rather resent is the implication that mental illness is hereditary. Possibly. Even I'm not an expert. But if so, very rarely. . . . One hears Marilyn Monroe was tormented by the thought of succumbing to mental illness, as her mother did. I find this appallingly fabricated."
—Gene Tierney, actress (*Laura*), who was temporarily institutionalized

"It's almost as though she had too much. Of looks, fame, fortune, and adulation. So, tear her down some. Or a lot. Particularly once she's dead and can't sue."
—Joey Bishop, entertainer and Rat Pack member

"Because she would ask a director what her character's motivation was, Marilyn was often ridiculed in the business and, when word got out about it, in the press. Sheer sexism! When Kim Novak asked Hitchcock about her motivation in *Vertigo*, he told her [that] her paycheck was her motivation and she was supposed to be a professional, so don't ask questions, just act. I doubt he would have replied the same way had James Stewart asked the question."
—Eva Dahlbeck, Swedish actress, *Smiles of a Summer Night*

"Some of the publicity about Marilyn Monroe, I feel, overstates her misery about failing to carry a pregnancy to term. As if those unsuccessful pregnancies made her feel such a failure that she resorted to suicide. If that were the case, you'd have millions of women bent on a suicidal course."
—Gene Siskel, film critic

"Marilyn's final birthday was June 1, 1962. Studios gave major stars elaborate birthday parties if they were filming, but Fox paid no attention to Marilyn [while shooting *Something's Got to Give*]. One excuse was that *Cleopatra* was bankrupting the studio, and they had put up with Elizabeth Taylor's bad behavior."   —Lois Banner, MM biographer

"More than anything else in her life, Marilyn Monroe wanted
to be taken seriously as an actress."
—Gloria Steinem

"I did a picture, *The Revolt of Mamie Stover*, that was thoroughly camouflaged to hide the fact that much of it took place in a Honolulu brothel. It was very controversial in 1956 . . . even its title. Mamie was the First Lady's name [Mamie Eisenhower]. . . . Marilyn had been offered the role but turned it down. She told [studio chief] Darryl Zanuck she didn't want to play a prostitute. He couldn't understand that, he was furious with her."
—Jane Russell

"When Marilyn became a star and asked to have some input into the making of her pictures, Zanuck swore that he would destroy her. That's the word he used."
—Ralph Roberts, masseur and friend

"Her studio refused to let her play dramatic roles. She wanted to do more serious things. They wanted her to keep repeating the gold-digger roles that brought in all that gold for the studio. Irony: Zanuck and company were the real gold diggers. Finally, Marilyn had to walk out on them and leave for the East Coast for them to admit that she meant business."
—David Shipman, Hollywood historian

"Miss Monroe was exceptionally beautiful. She was exceptionally successful in her profession. Yet I have read numerous comments by Americans saying they think she was a failure. How is this possible? Except for her early death, who would not want to be Marilyn Monroe? Including half of the male population." —Astrid Lindgren, Swedish author of the Pippi Longstocking books

"You'll find that most of those poor-sad-neurotic Marilyn books and articles are written by men. They have to find something wrong with her, sometimes to boost their own fragile or unfulfilled egos." —Rosie O'Donnell

CHAPTER 2

Vixen

"I think a big reason Marilyn is such an enduringly appealing, sexy icon is that she's one of few actresses who looks like she'd actually want and enjoy sex."   —Drew Barrymore

"She knew exactly what to do—her movements, her hands, her body were just perfect. She was the sexiest."

—Earl Moran, illustrator and pinup artist for whom MM posed early in her career

"She can make any move, any gesture, almost insufferably suggestive."

—Henry Hathaway, director, *Niagara*

"Sexy and erotic aren't really the same. Sexy should be fun—it's pleasure. Erotic can be forbidden. Or nasty. Or intimidating. Even unattainable. Erotic is usually what you can't get. Sexy is attainable."
—Michael Douglas

"Despite her beauty and popularity, Miss Monroe did not behave as if she'd just stepped down from a pedestal. . . . She was willing to shake a mere mortal's hand."

—Joe E. Brown, costar, *Some Like It Hot*

"Invariably being the center of attention, Marilyn had many distractions and concerns. But when she focused on you, she saw the individual and related to you. Even if only for thirty seconds, she made you feel special, and, afterward, you walked on air for thirty minutes."   —Cliff Harrington, American journalist based in Japan

"When she's there, she's there. All of her is there!"   —Clark Gable, costar, *The Misfits*

"Bodies are interchangeable, let's face it. Faces are not. Marilyn's face was everything. . . . Half the time, since she's died, you know, you only see her face. That's all you need."
                                                                          —Andy Warhol

"The luminosity of that face!"—Billy Wilder, director

"Hers is the sexiest face. Her eyes and lips clearly express desire. More than any face I've seen."   —Joe Namath, football star

"Because of her beauty, Marilyn wasn't allowed to be thought of as intelligent. That would be too much. And she certainly couldn't be political, not then. Yet the fact remains that she was very into books, was a committed liberal, and until the drugs took over, she was big into self-improvement."   —Shirley MacLaine

"It's the men who more resented, and maybe were threatened by, Monroe's looks. Women envied her, but some men, especially critics and journalists, seem to have resented her physical perfection. They had to try and bring her down for that."   —Oprah Winfrey

"Sexy, of course. But also: Marilyn wasn't threatening."   —Priscilla Presley

"Some pinup girls of the golden era looked seductive in a posed way. Marilyn Monroe was the most natural pinup. You got the feeling she wasn't posing, she just felt sexy."
                                                                —David Shipman, film historian

"I was watching TV, changing channels. . . . A young actress I've never heard of has, on the inside of her arm, this large tattoo of Marilyn Monroe's face! Amazing . . . on a girl. Outside of maybe a sailor, you'd never have seen such a tattoo on anybody during Marilyn's lifetime. She would be astounded."   —Dick Van Dyke, at a 2010 CD signing

"The hula girl in the grass skirt and Marilyn Monroe are the two most popular nonreligious female-illustration requests for tattoo artists in the Western world today [2008]."   —Len Jerome, Australian tattoo master

"The erotic hold that Marilyn exerts on people all over the world so many decades after her death is positively spooky."
        —Australian comedian Barry Humphries (aka [lilac-haired] Dame Edna Everage)

"This post-2000 vampire craze is something else.
For my money, the perfect vampire would be Marilyn Monroe.
Like, who wouldn't want to get bitten by her?"
—Brad Pitt, *Interview with the Vampire*

"Marilyn was the first star to appear nude in this country and get away with it. It was a side view, not full frontal, and a calendar shot, not moving-picture nudity, like Hedy Lamarr before her—and anyway, she was Austrian. Had this happened ten years earlier, Marilyn's career couldn't have recovered. But after WWII we were finally inching toward sexual freedom."

—Martin Ritt, director

"There was tremendous criticism, much of it hypocritical, about the nude calendar pose. Marilyn let it . . . speak for itself, let the furor die down. She said she'd done it to pay her bills, not to titillate. But titillate she definitely did! However she didn't seem calculating about it, so for the most part, she was forgiven."
—Gary Merrill, costar, *All About Eve*

"We may never know how much of Marilyn's comments just spilled out and how much was well-planned publicity. For instance, when the press asked what she wore to bed, she replied, 'Chanel No. 5.' That was both sexy and sounded the sort of thing she would say in all frankness."

—Evelyn Keyes, costar, *The Seven Year Itch*

"Of course Marilyn's movies made her a star. But two other factors helped push her so high. The nude calendar and her going with Joe DiMaggio. . . . He became the surrogate for all of America's sexually interested males."

—Art Linkletter, radio and TV host

"The nutty thing is, [DiMaggio] was sexually drawn to her, but once he had her, he was very jealous of her sexiness. If she had to be an actress, he didn't want her to be a sexy one. Can you believe it?"

—Susan Strasberg, actress and friend

"There were people who'd only heard about but never seen the nude photo that were nonetheless incensed about it. It was some new 'moral low' for the country. . . . A few of these people, once they saw Marilyn in a movie—and the calendar publicity did increase her box-office allure—that kind of softened them towards her."

—Joey Bishop, entertainer and Rat Pack member

"It was before my time, but I remember my father [actor Eddie Albert] thought it was 'brazen' of Marilyn Monroe to have appeared nude. Usually he said that when my mother was around. But he did become a fan, and we did go to see her movies. With my mom. Dad later said, 'It was just a case of youthful misjudgment.'"   —Edward Albert, actor

"When they put up a multistory-high billboard cutout of her in Times Square to advertise *The Seven Year Itch*, it was Marilyn in all her uninhibited glory, with the white dress blowing up toward her face. At that time, it wasn't just sexy, it was erotic and, to a big segment of the public, indecent. Joe flipped out. . . . It was the beginning of the end of Marilyn and Joe."   —Mike Connolly, gossip columnist

"Times change. Then, she was sexually very out there, pushing the envelope. What made it less outrageous was her little-girl quality, the wide-eyed innocence—real or acted. Today, Marilyn suggests, and promises, ecstasy."   —Paul Newman

"She is the ultimate temptress. But one who won't exact a high price or penalty. There's no dark side to her."
—Cameron Diaz

"People who knew her early on said Marilyn studied herself in the mirror like an exam. To perfect her public presentation and body language. Like the way she parted her lips in sort of an orgasmic expression. She knew what she was doing!"
—Angie Dickinson, actress rumored to have had an affair with JFK

"I'm sorry she's gone. But all I know is, she went around creating one controversy after another and milking it for all it was worth, and then getting more and more famous for it. Jeez! In my day, you had to have talent, not just bazooms."
—Ethel Merman, singer-actress, *There's No Business Like Show Business*

"A lot of Marilyn's 'moves' were given her by Jack Cole, the dancer-choreographer she worked closely with on her first several films. He was gay, but a hard taskmaster and very influential in his day, and he had final say on dance at the studio. . . . Before the cameras turned, he'd do the moves he wanted for Marilyn, like in the 'Diamonds Are a Girl's Best Friend' number, and then she'd copy him.

"There are those who say Jack invented Marilyn—an exaggeration. But her persona and way of moving, the gestures, she got a lot of those directly from Jack Cole."
—Gwen Verdon, actress-dancer who had been Cole's assistant

"Miss Monroe didn't issue frantic denials or contrite apologies when the nude calendar situation came to the fore. She kept her cool. It was her studio that was on the verge of canceling her contract."
—Wilfrid Hyde-White, costar, *Let's Make Love*

"Marilyn Monroe helped launch 'the sexual revolution.' With the nude shots and her suggestive walk . . . the very lipsticked, slightly open mouth and the half-closed dreamy eyelids. But obviously there was no movie nudity during her lifetime. Rather, once the '60s arrived, Marilyn did some seminude photo layouts. Do you know why? Because she was in her thirties and wanted proof that she was still alluring!"

—Sir Cecil Beaton, photographer-designer

"For her last [uncompleted] movie, *Something's Got to Give*, they shot a nighttime pool scene where Marilyn Monroe swam in the altogether. Some of it was printed in *Life* magazine. Nothing much showed, but it was the idea—it hadn't ever been done in a Hollywood film, and it was very sexy. Also very sad, because it was weeks before she died, and she never looked lovelier.

"When she finished the scene, she reportedly told her director, 'Not bad for thirty-six, huh?'"

—Dorothy Manners, gossip columnist

"Zanuck had gotten Marilyn on the casting couch, belittled her, underpaid her, then finally fired her. At the same time, he was bankrolling Liz Taylor in Rome, with endless delays in production that made *Cleopatra* the most expensive movie ever made and Liz the highest-paid star ever.

"But it was poor, vulnerable Marilyn who got fired, not fire-breathing Liz, who knew how to yell back."

—Sybil Brand, wife of Fox publicity chief Harry Brand

"When you think of Marilyn Monroe, or when I do,
two words come to mind. Beautiful. Vulnerable."
—Ellen DeGeneres

"When Marilyn was fired from her last picture, it wrecked her. Such a thing had never happened to a big star before, and she was already in bad shape, mentally. Not far from forty, she was as sexy as ever, yet believed her looks were almost gone, and if she didn't have them, then what? . . . It didn't take much to push her over the edge of the Hollywood cliff."
                                                        —George Cukor, director

"The thing with Marilyn that many photographers discovered is that she had an inner glow. She could light up from within, turn on the sex appeal, and draw every eye. . . . You might see her on the street, going about her business, and she wouldn't be that noticeable. But put her in front of a camera—it was like flicking a switch. The camera loved her, and she loved being loved."
                    —James Wong Howe, cinematographer

"It was disgusting, but the press was rather keen on her downward spiral—it sold a lot of newspapers and magazines."   —Robert Clary, actor (Frenchie on *Hogan's Heroes*)

"When they fired Marilyn Monroe, Fox's publicity department went to work, trying to make the studio look like the injured, abused party. Shameless! They'd ignored their star's very real health problems and objections to her film being drastically rewritten from under her.

"Fox may have done it for the publicity and to publicly shame Marilyn. Because soon afterward, but with minimal publicity, they renegotiated and hired her back—and on better terms."
                                                    —Richard Quine, writer-director

"Most everyone's seen the footage that remains of Marilyn from her uncompleted film, only a few months before her death. She was gorgeous . . . sexy, with a smile to melt your reserve . . . such charm, her sparkle. Then suddenly they put her light out. And Hollywood's gone downhill ever since."   —Jacqueline Susann, novelist

"Marilyn was better than her movies. They put her in things that made her a type of R-rated cartoon. Not X-rated, which didn't exist. If they'd put her into quality films of more mature sexuality, something like *Lady Chatterley's Lover* or any number of other things, she'd have been even better, even sexier. She was a national treasure handled by greedy incompetents."   —Jack Lemmon

"She didn't have to develop a sizzling persona. It was there in her first picture. Any time you see her on the silver screen, whether in a good, bad, or indifferent picture, she's the object of mental wolf whistles."
—Charlie Sheen

"The kid knew what she was doing. She was very body conscious . . . aware of her appeal and how to heighten it. Even literally. I saw a picture of her on the cover of one of them books. She's next to this other chick, they're on the beach, and the other chick's wearing some kind of sandal shoes. Marilyn's barefoot. They're smilin' at the camera, only Marilyn's pushing herself up like she has high heels on. To make her legs look better.
    "Oh, the kid knew. She always knew."
        —Rodney Dangerfield, actor-comedian (The book he mentions is *My Sister Marilyn* by half-sister Berniece Baker Miracle and her daughter Mona Rae Miracle.)

"Do you know Marilyn would often use at least three shades of lipstick to achieve her Look? She had it down pat, but to pull the whole dazzling thing together took time, and it's one reason she was often late for things. That, and—believe it or not—insecurity."

—Susan Strasberg, actress and daughter of MM's acting coach Lee Strasberg

"All I know is, if Marilyn Monroe was insecure about her appearance, what the hell chance do the rest of us have?"

—Sharon Tate

"I was named after the movie *Gilda*, a role Rita Hayworth played. That's bad enough. At least not that many people still remember that movie or Rita Hayworth in it. It would've been worse if they'd called me Marilyn."

—Gilda Radner, actress-comedian, *Saturday Night Live*

"There was a song I loved called 'I Want to Be Loved by You' which fascinated me. Not because of the music and not the words so much. Because it was sung for all times by Marilyn Monroe [in *Some Like It Hot*]. She made it sound like a girl, an innocent. But also she made it very seductive. It's wonderful!" —Sergio Franchi, singer

"On one of the *Gilligan's Island* episodes, Tina Louise sang 'I Wanna Be Loved by You' as Ginger Grant . . . a song Marilyn Monroe had recently popularized. I'm not sure whether Tina intended to do a distinct rendition, but it came off very Marilyn, which, as far as I was concerned, was delightful." —Sherwood Schwartz , the series's creator-writer-producer

"Tina Louise and I didn't always see eye to eye [on *Gilligan's Island*]. Not so much because she wanted to be the star. It's mostly that Ginger, her character, didn't really fit our show. It was a situation comedy. Lots of kids watched, and it was for all ages. It wasn't meant to be sexy. All our characters were asexual, if you want to put it that way. Even the Howells. I always felt what Tina was doing was better for motion pictures. Tina even copied Marilyn Monroe's voice and once said Ginger was a cross between Marilyn and Lucille Ball."

—Bob "Gilligan" Denver

"Up until *Gilligan's Island*, one of the high points of my life was doing scenes with Marilyn Monroe. She played a secretary in a movie called *Home Town Story* [1951]. It came and went, nothing really special. Till after Marilyn became a star. . . . She played a somewhat aloof young lady, but as an actress and a person, Marilyn was charming. When she smiled, I just about buckled at the knees."

—Alan "Skipper" Hale Jr.

"Marilyn didn't need to churn out two or three films a year to keep in the public eye. Her private life and appearances, coupled with ongoing public interest, kept her on top. It's surprising how few pictures she did do after she became a star. Several on the way up of course, but fewer as a star than any comparable male star."

—Radie Harris, newspaper columnist

"Box office is everything. Marilyn had been off the screen for quite a while and in her new movie she had a smallish role, though with No. 1 billing. Tinseltown was suggesting she was washed up. But then *Some Like It Hot* became her biggest hit. Monroe was back on top. But it was her last hit."

—Oleg Cassini, friend and fashion designer

"I like Miss Monroe, sure. But I wouldn't care to take my wife and family to see her at the movies. She's adult fare, basically for men only. That's fine. I don't think she should be banned, as long as she stays on the big screen and within the bounds of good taste and decency. . . . Some things you can't get on television, and shouldn't get on television."
—Richard Denning, actor best known as the governor on TV's *Hawaii Five-O*

"The sexual exuberance of that woman was, and is, unmatched on screen."
—Terence Young, director of three James Bond movies

"There was a 1950s radio preacher who called Marilyn Monroe 'a pernicious sexual influence.' Opposing her growing fame was his publicity gimmick. As if she was causing the downfall of Western civilization. Which reminds me of the snotty English journalist who asked Mahatma Gandhi when he visited England, 'What do you think of English civilization?' The saintly little Indian replied, 'I think it would be an excellent idea.'

"Anyhow, turns out this preacher, in his garage, had a box full of Marilyn's nude calendar shots, apart from a load of pornographic books. It reminds me of preachers and politicians who rant and rave against gay rights, and then some get caught with a male hustler."
—Donald Rawley, *Buzz* magazine editor

"Marilyn Monroe's influence on US actresses has not been good insofar as voice is concerned. Too many young actresses have tried to imitate her breathy delivery. . . . They can't usually be heard, and it's unsuitable for most dramatic roles. What such a whispery voice conveys is, 'Don't take me seriously.'"
—Michael Shurtleff, acting coach

"Larry Olivier told an associate that he couldn't act with Marilyn Monroe if she continued to use 'that voice.' Which voice did he think she was going to use? What Larry really disliked was that *The Prince and the Showgirl* was based on Terry Rattigan's play *The Sleeping Prince*, to which Monroe had bought the screen rights. It was the first movie from Marilyn Monroe Productions."
                                                    —Laurence Harvey, British actor

"Olivier was sexually intimidated by Marilyn Monroe. He directed the picture but evidently felt swamped by her. He was used to more sedate British actresses and was, truth to tell, a closeted bisexual. He'd rather have worked opposite a more decorous, less buxom type like Audrey Hepburn."
                        —Sydney Chaplin (Charlie's son), actor

"When Marilyn and Sir Laurence Olivier held a press conference promoting their upcoming film, I was one of between one hundred and two hundred journalists and photographers in attendance. . . . Sir Laurence was rather stiff and not very demonstrative toward his future costar, despite encouragement. Marilyn was happy to be there, confident and able to deal with some inane questions about setting up her own production company, which very few female stars had done.

"At one strategic point, Marilyn stole the spotlight and created a marvelous photo opportunity when one of the straps of her gown broke. She was so sweetly and disarmingly embarrassed, although all that was showing was her bare shoulder. However, pandemonium broke out among the photographers, and the next day she starred—minus Sir Laurence—in newspaper photos that circled the globe.

"Of course it had been arranged, and I already had a safety pin to lend Marilyn after her strap 'broke.'"
                                        —Judith Crist, journalist and film critic

"In 1998 the dress which Marilyn Monroe wore when she sang 'Happy Birthday' to President Kennedy sold for $1.26 million."
 —Lois W. Banner, author of *MM–Personal: From the Private Archive of Marilyn Monroe*

"I saw Marilyn Monroe in *The Prince and the Showgirl*. She was absolutely fabulous! She was over thirty, and that was when they thought thirty was over the hill for an actress. But it's as if she amped up her beauty and her star-glow in it. . . . She was a consummate comedienne."
                                                                                        —Anne Hathaway

"When she appeared in public, she catered to the public, to what they expected. How else could she dress? Unfortunately, clothes also make the woman, and by dressing the way she did—like a vixen, provocatively—she undercut the image she was trying to amend. If you wear clothes like that, you don't get mistaken for a serious dramatic actress."
                                                                —Derek Anson Jones, theater director

"On Marilyn Monroe, when you look at pictures of her, the clothes never wear her. Occasionally, you hardly notice them. It's her face you notice, and sometimes her pose or a gesture. Certainly her expression . . . such an expressive face."
—Sandra Bullock

"I did a movie, *Those Lips, Those Eyes*. Someone asked me if it was about Marilyn Monroe. Possibly if I'd gone around saying yes, more people would have seen it."   —Frank Langella

"Her lips are a national monument."   —Lenny Bruce, comedian

"No one has worn lipstick as sensationally as Marilyn Monroe has. It makes me sometimes want to give up."
—Sandra Dee

"Some professional predecessors informed me that Marilyn practiced many a time in front of her mirror, perfecting that half-open-mouth pose and the beautiful shape it made." —Way Bandy, makeup artist

"Hers are the most famous lips in history." —Blake Edwards, director

"Excuse my bad writing in English, I have bought and read Croatian copy of your book translated from *Hollywood Babble On*. I liked reading it and very much have liked on the cover the beautiful lips of movie star Marilene [*sic*] Monroe."
—from a 1997 letter to this author

"Marilyn did the eyes thing so well. . . . Often, she'd look at the camera with half-closed eyes, as if she were having a sexy daydream. It came across as semi-erotic and was a new phenomenon. Don't think she didn't get ostracized for that! But it sold. . . . Look at the celluloid sirens before her. When they looked toward the camera, it was more straightforward, more daytime. Marilyn was nighttime." —Kenn Duncan, photographer

"There was one blonde precursor to Marilyn Monroe who was as frankly suggestive as she, but that was Mae West, who didn't, ahem, grace the screen until she was about forty."
—John Huston, director, *The Misfits*

"In the 1970s or thereabouts, actresses started intimating a bedroom look by posing with disheveled hair. In Marilyn Monroe's era, that wasn't done—people would have called it messy or lazy . . . unladylike. Marilyn could suggest that fresh-out-of-the-bedroom—or let's go into the bedroom—mystique with her eyes and lips. She was signaling an invitation and perking up the male audience. That made her a star."   —Angela Lansbury

"Maybe I'm peculiar, but where other moviegoers looked at Marilyn Monroe and drooled, I looked at her and listened to her, and I laughed. Her comic timing . . . she was instinctually gifted. She never lost what most children lose when they grow up—which I won't even try and define."
—Imogene Coca, comic actress

"One memorable challenge I had was to show off Marlene Dietrich, not young but still slim, to tremendous advantage on the Las Vegas stage, with an illusion of near nudity. That helped prepare me for the gown Marilyn Monroe wore to the forty-fifth birthday party for President John F. Kennedy at Madison Square Garden in May 1962. About twenty thousand people attended the fund-raiser.

"It was rumored that the gown cost about $15,000, a tremendous sum for a dress then. But the cost is unimportant. It looked perfect on her. It was formfitting and gave the seminude impression. Miss Monroe was sewn into the gown standing up—not that she couldn't sit in it. . . . It was flesh-colored and had sequins and beads, but the illusion was that she wore nothing beneath them."   —Jean Louis, designer

"I think Marilyn Monroe has the most magnetic face in movie history. It's not easy to remove your gaze."
—Neil Patrick Harris

"Several years after Marilyn died, someone asked me on a radio show what ever happened to the tan loafers I wore in *The Seven Year Itch*. I didn't know what the guy was talking about. He said he would give almost anything to be in the same shoes as the man who stood next to Marilyn Monroe in the infamous white-dress scene. He asked again, and I said I didn't know what happened to the shoes. I hadn't even remembered what color they were.

"After that, I got several inquiries about the shoes, but I wasn't sure if I'd gotten to keep them or if they stayed studio property. All I know is, each time someone offered me money for the shoes, the price kept going up and up. . . . I sure wish I had those damn shoes today. I could maybe retire on them."

—Tom Ewell

"If she'd been a brunette star, I think those nude photos would have seriously harmed or ended her career. A brunette or a haughty or a dramatic actress. But our Marilyn . . . she took that taboo, turned it around, and made it work for her!"
—Eddie Fisher, singer who married Elizabeth Taylor, two blonde stars, and a Chinese millionairess

"When the shots of Marilyn that became a best-selling calendar were made public, her rising star could have been shot down then and there. That was the McCarthy era, politically insane and sexually still very repressed. . . . Marilyn acted as if her body was a natural thing and showing it was not a crime. She was right on both counts."

—Peter Lawford, actor and JFK in-law

"Remember the Miss America who denied she'd ever been photographed nude or seminude? Why deny photographic evidence? Like the two-time Oscar-winning actor who's been photographed canoodling with a man in his car and still says he's not gay. Dumb, dumb, dumb! Marilyn Monroe was smart. She admitted it, didn't do a big song and dance about it, and above all didn't act proud or flippant. Her photos faded into the background, so to speak, and she got on with her business."
—Joan Rivers

"It was touch and go. Was this the end of Marilyn Monroe? Fortunately, America forgave her for posing nude. More importantly, so did Hollywood."

—Shelley Winters, actress and one-time roommate

"When the arrest records for Farrah Fawcett and another blonde from TV came out and revealed they'd done shoplifting years before, many people were very disappointed. Half believed their stories—you know, the person usually says it was all a misunderstanding— and half were disgusted with their morality. But stealing is one thing. Doing a nude camera session is another. It's nowhere as mercenary."

—Anne Jackson, actress, friend, and wife of *The Misfits* costar Eli Wallach

"When that famous actress was caught shoplifting, big-time, an elderly friend of mine compared it to Marilyn Monroe when her nude photo went public. I was surprised and asked what's that got to do with it? There's really no comparison, I said. Shoplifting is selfish. It's a small-spirited act. Being photographed without clothes is not."

—Philip Seymour Hoffman

"There've always been rumors about stars doing porn, going way back. Usually women . . . Joan Crawford, a 'stag film,' I think. Sylvester Stallone did in point of fact do a porno. I think if Marilyn Monroe had had a straitlaced image and then the nude photos were discovered, it would have damaged her irreparably. But she was a deliberately sexy blonde; it didn't come as a huge surprise, did it? And the result was not only fetching but rather discreet–certainly by today's standards." —Hugh Grant

"Marilyn explained that she'd posed as a struggling starlet and needed the money, about fifty bucks, to pay her rent. It was believable and probably true." —Geoffrey Beene, fashion designer

"Jane Russell could sympathize with Miss Monroe because she'd been a victim of media hype and salacious photos herself. This was a few years before Marilyn's fiasco, and Jane didn't bare anything. But her bosom was emphasized as no actress's ever had been, thanks to Howard Hughes. He decided to make the newcomer an instant star, and for *The Outlaw* he devised special bras for Jane and fed the publicity mills endless photos of her cleavage.

"If the powerful Hughes, who bought RKO studios, hadn't been behind that travesty, it would have terminated Russell's career. He marketed *The Outlaw* like it was X-rated, but it was just a western whose main theme was male jealousy—of another man. Besides, Jane, like Marilyn, had a sense of humor. So the scandal passed and her career climbed. In spite of that tasteless man."

—John Cromwell, director and father of actor James Cromwell

"After the Second World War, things began changing so fast . . . an example was Marilyn Monroe's calendar pose. Before the war, that would've stopped any girl's acting efforts cold. The photographs with just the top half or two-thirds of Jane Russell's breasts made it doubtful she'd ever get another acting job. . . . With Marilyn Monroe, all kinds of people were now speaking up on her behalf. I was one of 'em. I didn't happen to think it was the end of the world."
                                                    —Jack Buetel, actor, *The Outlaw*

"You can be sure that after the Monroe nude-photo scandal, actresses kept buttoned up and stayed away from photographers with seedy reputations. *She* got away with it, but it would have been a professional kiss of death for most. Of course nowadays actresses know their careers won't suffer . . . if anything, they'll reap a heap of publicity if it comes out."
                                        —Suzanne Pleshette, actress, *The Bob Newhart Show*

"There have been actresses who had nude shots made, then secretly arranged for them to be publicly released, pretending like they're shocked and mortified and, oh dear, those shots were *never* intended for public consumption. Oh-gee-golly!"
                             —Whoopi Goldberg

"There's a photographer in London who specializes in private 'romance pictorials,' where the female subject assumes the same poses Marilyn Monroe did. His clients vary in background and include oil-rich Arabs who want their bleached-blonde girlfriends—the wives are typically brown-haired—to try and follow in Marilyn's footsteps, as it were. It's an aphrodisiac thing and rather pathetic."
                                                                —Sir Alan Bates

"In Hollywood today, some actresses just starting out go the dubious route of posing topless or nude. Perhaps they think it'll give them some reflected Marilyn Monroe limelight. It's mostly about vanity and is sort of an acknowledgment of lack of talent. . . . Whether Marilyn was really hard up for the money or whether it was a vanity thing, who knows? Or some combination of the two."   —John Alonzo, cinematographer, *The Godfather*

"When you've been making the rounds, auditioning for roles and not getting them . . . when your contract is cancelled . . . when Hollywood heartbreak is at its roughest and a would-be actress feels she's probably not good enough or attractive enough to make it, an offer to pose au naturel because you're so good-looking must be almost irresistible."
—Bud Fraker, Hollywood photographer

"Miss Monroe had comedic talent and developed her camera presence. Initially, she was in that vast category of employability-by-way-of-looks, which most female newcomers fall into. As opposed to the talent category. Talent lasts longer and increases with time. The limited shelf life on the good looks of any actress may lead her to do unwise things that can stall a career or shatter an image.

"I did think at the time that those nudies would do Marilyn Monroe in. . . . I'm glad they didn't."   —Bette Davis

"What gets me is how Hugh Hefner would every so often include photos of Marilyn [in *Playboy*] and label it as a tribute. Not sheer, crass commercialism."   —Valerie Harper

"There's one US movie star who, while new to the business, let this guy, maybe he was her boyfriend, take all these seminude photos of her. Eventually she hits stardom, and the guy, who legally owns the negatives, decides to publish one—I think just one. So she sues him and the judge finds in her favor and the guy's banned from ever publishing another. But after all, she's the one who agreed to do it in the first place. Nobody forced her, and I say it's bloody unfair."

—Sir Michael Caine

"The man who took the pictures ended up making a lot more money for his easy job than poor Marilyn did. But the one who made by far the most was Hugh Hefner, by exploiting Marilyn Monroe in his *Playboy* magazine. He made minimum a million dollars off her."

—Canadian actress Lois Maxwell (aka Miss Moneypenny in fourteen James Bond movies)

"The bottom line is those photos were not all that shocking. The most shocking thing you saw then, in the '50s, was nipples. Or a nipple—the side view. Had pubic hair been involved, yes, that would have been a capital-S scandal and a finale."

—Marvin Hamlisch composer

"Ingrid Bergman was playing good girls and Joan of Arc before she became pregnant by an Italian director while she was married to a Swedish doctor. America turned against her. They felt betrayed. Americans like to think you are what you play—or they did then. . . . Marilyn Monroe was a sex symbol. She didn't betray anyone—and pleased very many."

—Penelope Cruz

"If Marilyn had been a more calculating type . . . but she had the prototypical dumb-blonde image. She seemed guileless. Much of the public reacted to the nudity issue by making excuses for 'dear dumb Marilyn,' as if she'd just made a bad choice or some scheming photographer managed to talk her into it. Marilyn was likable, and that saved her ass, to put it bluntly."

—Woody Allen

"Marilyn was not the first so-called dumb blonde. Marie Wilson had made a profitable career in the 1940s out of playing dumb on radio and in movies [such] as *My Friend Irma*. Even in the '50s Marilyn wasn't alone. That decade of economic progress and social and political backsliding was rife with dumb blondes.

"But the fact that Marilyn wasn't ruined by posing nude was a turning point . . . an early strike for the sexual revolution."

—Jack Kroll, *Newsweek* writer, editor

"The difference between Marilyn and Jayne Mansfield is a matter of extremes, and America usually opts for the non-extreme. Marilyn was more lovely of face, while Jayne had the bigger bust—in some opinions, too big. And while Marilyn didn't come off as an intellectual, Jayne sometimes came off as the next thing to an idiot. Even then it was sort of sad, but it's what Jayne chose to keep doing."

—Skip E. Lowe, cable TV talk-show host

"With Jayne Mansfield, you could see the naked ambition. You saw through her publicity stunts. For her, there was no such thing as bad publicity. Marilyn was far more natural and ingenuous. She seemed to be having a good time. Jayne seemed always on the lookout for a lens or a cameraman."

—Robert Mitchum

"Everyone was talking as if Marilyn and I were having an affair, which was jolly flattering but complete nonsense. When we got home, Marilyn's lawyer was waiting for me, full of dire threats, but Marilyn rose to her full height and told him that if he lifted a little finger against me, it would be him who got fired, not me."
—Colin Clark, British author of *My Week with Marilyn*

"Early on there were some planted rumors of an affair between Miss Monroe and Sir Laurence. Both were married . . . [but] it was he who did nothing to discourage the rumors. If anything, they shored up the purely heterosexual illusion he was always anxious to promote. . . . The rumors abated when it became known he couldn't stand her and was eager to shine at her expense. He didn't like being in the same room with her."
—Richard Wattis, costar, *The Prince and the Showgirl*

"One story, unverified but widespread, is that even Vivien Leigh [then Olivier's wife] found Marilyn beautiful and sexy, which she was. Vivien had starred in the play on which the film was based, so it wasn't the most comfortable situation. . . . But she wasn't worried about a possible liaison between Sir Laurence and Marilyn.

"Vivien was intrigued that Marilyn had a bisexual reputation in the business—not in public, of course. Being past her prime she didn't relish being photographed next to Marilyn. She kept her distance but asked certain people about Marilyn's possible liaisons with such as Barbara Stanwyck, Joan Crawford, and Marilyn's ex-coach Natasha Lytess. Vivien enjoyed hearing—just hearing—about that aspect of things."
—C. David Heymann, MM biographer

"Larry costarred with Marilyn Monroe, but he had to be her director. It meant he was in control and could presumably control her. It accorded him prestige—the great English thespian overseeing an American star. . . . Larry was keenly aware that this motion picture was being produced by a Hollywood studio and by his costar's company. Aware and irritated."

—Sir John Gielgud

"I imagine Laurence Olivier found Marilyn appealing, as almost anyone would, including some gay actors I know. The lady had charm to spare, which didn't mean you wanted to be the latest man to sleep with her, but I think jealousy got the better of Olivier. He didn't want to be outdone by a Hollywood personality, not by a woman star, and especially not by—as he once called her at a party—Little Miss No-Talent."

—Rock Hudson

"I never went to bed with Marilyn Monroe, and I'll be damned if I'm going to sit around listening to other chaps who didn't lying their heads off saying they did."
—Oliver Reed, British actor, *Oliver!*

"Strange thing about a woman who is both beautiful and, in vulgar parlance, a sex bomb. The men around her will watch and wait for any sign of personal interest, irregardless what they themselves look like. In addition, they watch her reactions to other men, all the more fiercely if a given man is good-looking. All this futile activity merely yields an impression of animalistic competition."

—Dame Edith Sitwell, British poet and critic

"One thing I noticed early on in the entertainment field is how the level of appreciation for a woman's looks and sex appeal is countered, for most men, by their level of contempt. Like they resent her for turning them on. . . . If you're somebody like a Marilyn Monroe, you can have a certain degree of sexual power over men. But the dominant side of the coin is that men control all the money and major decisions in this business, so I don't see why they have to be so contemptuous."

—Lesley Gore, singer-songwriter, "It's My Party"

"I got to actually visit the set of *Gentlemen Prefer Blondes*. Jane Russell was sort of one of the guys, but Marilyn Monroe was . . . Marilyn Monroe! Wow-wow. When she appeared on set, some of the guys' tongues were practically hanging out of their mouths. Others were acting nonchalant—you know, like 'Oh, well, she's not so much.' I found the contrast interesting."
—anonymous friend of Peter Hawks, son of director Howard Hawks

"Politics and sex were very risky topics during the '50s, and most of Marilyn's career took place during that benighted time. Like most actresses, she was liberally inclined but kept silent. Standing by and then marrying Arthur Miller was a courageous political act, but one defensibly cloaked in romance and marriage.

"It was in the sphere of sexuality that Marilyn Monroe pushed the boundaries, visibly and publicly. Religious groups and those fearsome women's clubs were still powerful, but Marilyn's success and her popular acceptance went a long way toward eroding the power and intimidation they'd so long practiced."

—Dalton Trumbo, blacklisted screenwriter

"I don't think Marilyn starred in a single movie that today would come close to an R-rating. PG, maybe. But I had friends whose parents wouldn't let them go see a Marilyn Monroe movie because they thought she was too sexy for kids to see."
—Natalie Wood

"I don't know whether most young people today see the FBI in a positive or a negative light, but its history was provably anti-democracy. They collected files on anyone they disliked or deemed a threat to the nation, including Hollywood stars like Marilyn Monroe. . . . There was plenty against her in their eyes, because she was a media sensation and married influential men. [FBI chief] J. Edgar Hoover feared that someday she might give an interview and make a political comment. And worse, that people would listen."
—Charles Guggenheim, Oscar-winning documentary filmmaker, *Robert Kennedy Remembered*

"I remember when the Beatles arrived on the American scene. . . . Being English and long-haired, they ignited the fears of groups who warned against their influence on American youth—basically, that the Beatles might turn American boys gay. One far-right columnist even said the Beatles were probably all gay, because their manager Brian Epstein was gay and Jewish—he of course mentioned Jewish.

"These same groups were harassing Marilyn Monroe a few years earlier. First, when it came out about her posing nude for the still camera, and then when she married a left-wing Jewish writer [Arthur Miller]. She posed a 'real and imminent danger,' seducing men of all ages and corrupting innocent girls who wanted to dye their hair blonde and live like Marilyn Monroe. It seems funny now. It was not funny then."
—William Gibson, playwright, *The Miracle Worker*

"America has given us several sexy actresses, but the first sexual American actress is Marilyn Monroe. Sexy *and* sexual. Despite that, Mademoiselle Monroe, unlike a continental actress, will probably never disrobe for the [movie] camera."

–Jacques Brel, Belgian singer-songwriter

"Her publicity was often crude–the way she was promoted for public consumption. Like a juicy piece of meat dangled in front of a ravenous lion. . . . The promoters treated every moviegoer as if he or she was a sex-starved heterosexual male. Of course Marilyn herself was never crude."

–George Nader, gay actor

"Oh, I loved Marilyn! What a delight she was. I realize she was being pitched to the gentlemen, but . . . ladies of a certain persuasion loved Marilyn–in both senses of the word."

–Nancy Kulp (aka Jane Hathaway on *The Beverly Hillbillies*)

"Ladies are prettier than menfolk, and I always liked the prettiest. That was Marilyn Monroe. She was the top, like in the Cole Porter song. Marilyn was 'the impossible dream' that a lot of us sepia ladies liked to dream about. It didn't come better than that."

–Nellie Lutcher, singer who at age eleven was playing piano for Ma Rainey, "Mother of the Blues"

"Being a teenage girl with a crush on Marilyn Monroe isn't a lesbian thing, it's understandable and sensible. How can anyone possibly criticize that?"

–Megan Mullally, actress, *Will and Grace*

"Some fans get crushes on more threatening figures like Brando or Bardot or Elvis. Some go for a nonthreatening sex symbol . . . like Marilyn Monroe. I think with her it's more of a romantic crush."   —Emma Thompson, actor-writer (with Oscars for both)

"The thing with Marilyn is that a woman can find her attractive, even sexually attractive, and still regard her as an icon, a sister, a friend, as somebody they identify with even if their looks and life situation don't resemble Marilyn's at all."

—Kathy Najimy, actress, *Sister Act*

"Marilyn Monroe is a rare example of a star who was ideally beautiful that a woman doesn't have to feel jealous of. Today's women can feel for her in a way that women of her own era did not. Women were more programmed to dislike each other. There was minimal solidarity then."
—Elaine Stritch

"Marilyn's one of the few female stars you can vicariously turn on to without feeling guilty about it. Like, who doesn't think she's a turn-on?"

—Lili Taylor, actress, *I Shot Andy Warhol*

"I discovered Anna Freud's findings when she analyzed Marilyn during a week in London in 1956. According to Anna [daughter of Sigmund], Marilyn was bisexual."

—Dr. Lois Banner, PhD and MM researcher and biographer

"Marilyn Monroe is in the habit of shocking the American public. That is probably not a bad thing."

—Kurt Goldstein, neurologist-psychiatrist

"Marilyn Monroe gave a genuine quote that was shockingly honest for its time—and ours, or else it would be famous. I quote: 'A man who had kissed me once had said it was very possible I was a lesbian because I apparently had no response to males—meaning him. I didn't contradict him because I didn't know what I was.'

"What an incredibly revealing and candid admission. Talk about courageous. Even if she guessed her comment would scarcely be reproduced anywhere. Then or now. Check out the quote yourself. That woman is my hero!" —k. d. lang, Canadian singer-songwriter

"All the girls knew who was for other women in La-La Land and which marriages were phony—matri-phony, and there's still plenty of it, usually for the boys. . . . The true frisson for a lezzie and for some straight guys was the inside scoop on Marilyn Monroe and that Russian acting coach she lived with and brought onto the soundstages of all her movies."   —Patsy Kelly, openly gay comic actress

"The directors who objected to the presence and the required approval of Natasha Lytess were probably jealous of her. Probably assumed she got to sleep with Marilyn. A man director wants total control of his cast, especially his leading lady. With no competition."
—Arthur Laurents, playwright, director, and screenwriter

"One of the bigger Hollywood mysteries was why Marilyn and Natasha split up. Almost inseparable one day, then . . . phfft! It couldn't have been Fox, because they'd already tried breaking them up, and Marilyn stood firm. . . . Did Natasha suddenly go too far? But how far would too far have to be, with two females? Unless she was going to go public. I doubt it. Who knows?"   —Charles Nelson Reilly, actor and acting coach

"Lytess was a mystery woman. Where'd she come from, what did she really do? And I heard she was German, not Russian. . . . Natasha didn't seem to want publicity or fame . . . she just seemed to want Marilyn.

"After Marilyn, she seemed to just disappear, and you couldn't hardly find out why or where . . . you couldn't google anything then. Even now, you can only find out so much, and there's still plenty of covering up."   —Maxene Andrews of the Andrews Sisters

"A few individuals wondered if Lytess had some hold over Monroe, knew something about her past. I think it was less nefarious than that. She was a helper who cared about Marilyn as a person. And if there was any sex involved, she didn't demean Marilyn the way various men had. Personally, I like men, but between two women, they're peers, in a way you almost never find between a man and a woman—ever in that order, according to myth and custom."   —Sheree North, actress hired by Twentieth Century Fox
as a "threat" and possible replacement for MM

"Natasha was with Marilyn almost from her career's inception. Their relationship ran from 1948 to 1953, the year Marilyn's superstardom was confirmed at the box office. During those years Natasha helped Marilyn to gain confidence and gave her the tools to act. . . . Obviously when Marilyn broke through big-time in 1953, pressure was applied to drop Natasha for Marilyn's image and her long-term acceptance by Middle America."
—Dr. Betty Berzon, psychologist and author

"It may well be that Marilyn Monroe wanted to avoid a sapphic reputation that would harm her public image and limit her roles. The repertoire afforded her was already pretty limited."   —Jackie Cooper, actor-director, speculating on MM's split with Natasha Lytess

"Natasha Lytess may have begun acting like a possessive husband. That's my guess. Look how Marilyn and Joe [DiMaggio] were through in less than a year once he began acting like a possessive husband. I think Marilyn made the right choice in both cases."

—Bob Carroll Jr., cowriter, *I Love Lucy*

"Another of Marilyn Monroe's tragedies is that if she were bisexually inclined and in love with a woman, she'd have had at all costs to hide it. There was no 'lesbian chic' then, just bigotry and reprisal. So instead of possibly being happy with a woman, she had to go through grief with a series of men—husbands and lovers—who done her wrong."

—Amanda Donohoe, actress, *L.A. Law*

"When you're new or relatively new to the scene, you can get away with a certain amount of nonconformity. But superstardom means mass stardom, and you have to not only appeal to the masses but conform to their standards. So if Marilyn was, so to speak, flaunting her female acting advisor as a new star, once she became a superstar she'd have to dance to the majority tune."

—Ira Levin, author-screenwriter-playwright, *Rosemary's Baby*

"Apparently Marilyn had a healthy sexual curiosity. She didn't see sex or the human body in terms of sin. Yet Hollywood, which exploits sex for profit, is an institution that backs the socioreligious norm."

—Cynthia Nixon, actress, *Sex and the City*

"One can see in her performances and even the way she wore clothes that Marilyn enjoyed her body and enjoyed other people enjoying it. She was, truly, a sensuous woman."

—Judy Carne, actress, *Rowan & Martin's Laugh-In*

"Anything can be interpreted in at least two ways. It's true, Marilyn was supremely comfortable in front of a photographic but not a motion-picture camera. . . . Toward the end of her life, when she posed topless behind a gauzy scarf, you could offer that as proof of her evolving sexual honesty or say that she was reduced to more blatant publicity because her movie career was in the doldrums.

"The other reigning sex symbol of the period, Elizabeth Taylor, never exposed her breasts. Maybe she was uptight or . . . didn't have to. Any time Liz wanted extra publicity, all she had to do was get a new husband—often somebody else's!"

—Kenn Duncan, photographer

"Some of the early gowns Marilyn wore to premieres and the like were on the exhibitionistic side and slightly tacky. Her taste improved with time. After a certain point, she didn't have to force the camera's attention. . . . The camera came to her, and it could emphasize her looks, not her costume or her cleavage."

—Ray Aghayan, costume designer

"I don't recall off the bat who designed our costumes for *There's No Business Like Show Business*, but brother! The getups they hung on Marilyn Monroe. Godawful. Gaudy . . . and awful. I think it wasn't till she got the power of veto that she wore clothes where you didn't stare at them and could just zero in on her natural beauty."   —Dan Dailey, costar

"I was flattered by the comparison . . . and somewhat afraid of it. I didn't feel my hair color should pigeonhole me, and as a person I'm very different from Marilyn Monroe."

—Carroll Baker, actress, *Baby Doll*

"In terms of her look, there's early Marilyn and late Marilyn, sometimes called hard Marilyn and soft Marilyn, when she had a less made-up face and the lipstick wasn't fire-engine red. She looked fantastic with much of her early look, but it was literally painted on. Like in *Niagara*, where she's killed off because she's cheating on her husband. The more villainous a character was, the more makeup they buried her under."

—Kevyn Aucoin, makeup artist

"In the 1960s it was a new, fresher-looking Marilyn. A natural Marilyn, less manufactured. It was a time of turning away from old norms . . . and makeup changed radically. Unlike some stars who hang on to their trademark makeup and hairdos forever, Marilyn embraced the new look, and it suited her beautifully."

—George Sidney, director, *Show Boat*

"Marilyn's physical aspect shifted, for the better. It's too bad her roles stayed in the same rut. She looked more modern but had to act the same old-fashioned chick parts. That whole male-chauvinist-oink-oink studio setup stank. Or stunk. Both!"
—Judy Tenuta, comedian-actress

"As time passed, I was glad I wasn't blonde, because that automatically put you in a precarious boat. The vessel's queen was Marilyn Monroe, no question, but how often it capsized. Look at the fates of so many blonde actresses, from Jean Harlow and Carole Landis to Marilyn and Sharon Tate. It's almost as if there's an instability in that hair color—an unreal color that typically comes from a bottle."

—Ruth Roman, actress, *Strangers on a Train*

"I worked in Hollywood, but producers there were afraid of foreign blondes. American blondes, they could tame. I was promoted as a cold, Swedish sexual tigress. I went to Italy to do my most famous work, in *La Dolce Vita*. Hollywood thought I might be the next Marilyn Monroe, but I didn't want to fit inside a mold. There was one Marilyn Monroe, and there is one Anita Ekberg. Why are they so fond of clones?"   —Anita Ekberg

"Hollywood is forever attempting to duplicate profits. They love you if you can walk in the gilded footsteps of a previous box-office champ. After [Rudolph] Valentino died, there was a parade of would-be 'Latin lovers' that lasted for decades, and even while Marilyn Monroe was alive there was an ongoing stream of new Marilyns who merely had to be blonde and not flat-chested.

"When originality happens, it's in spite of, not because of, Hollywood."
—Walter Matthau

"Later in the [1960s], an actress like Jane Fonda could transition from pretty-girl assignments to challenging dramas like *They Shoot Horses, Don't They?* Marilyn didn't get that chance. Perhaps if she'd lived a few years longer. . . ."   —Gene Siskel, film critic

"For my first movie, Jack Warner wanted to dye my hair, put me in a
corset, add falsies, break and reset my jaw so it would have a softer line,
and I don't know what else. Every studio wanted its own version of
Marilyn Monroe. . . . I don't think the Warners and Mayers and Zanucks,
et cetera, were satisfied with what any woman originally looked like."
—Jane Fonda

"One of Marilyn Monroe's favorites was Rita Hayworth, whose deserved nickname was the Love Goddess. Marilyn loved her in *Gilda*. . . . She admired her soft, cultivated speaking voice, also Rita's dancing talent. I don't know if Marilyn knew Rita began as a dancer. I heard Marilyn was confident of her own singing but not her dancing. . . . Marilyn took her mother's last name, possibly influenced by Rita, whose Irish mother was Haworth [*sic*].

   "Both lovely ladies ended up legendary and tragically—but *after* they'd achieved spectacular careers. Did you know the word 'spectacular' comes from an ancient word meaning 'to look at'? In both cases you couldn't choose anything better to look at."

—Glenn Ford, actor and frequent Hayworth costar

"Marilyn was enthralled when Rita Hayworth became the first American princess, when she married the son of that Aga Khan whatever-he-was. When Grace Kelly snagged Prince Rainier of Monaco, Marilyn asked a friend if there were any eligible princes left."

—Shelley Winters, actress and one-time roommate

"In *Gentlemen Prefer Blondes* Marilyn wore a diamond tiara. She loved how it looked and asked me if I thought wearing one to a public function would be appropriate. I didn't think she needed it. I didn't say some people would resent it; she already looked fantastic. Marilyn took my advice."

—Travilla, the film's costume designer

   "White was definitely her color. Like a lightbulb, and Marilyn provided the incandescent magic."

—Helen Rose, costume designer

"I could dine out free for the rest of my life thanks to the pleated white dress I put Marilyn Monroe in. . . . It was easy to do, there's little to say about it. I've designed hundreds, even hundreds and hundreds, of dresses. None got as much publicity or was modeled so well."
—Travilla

"Any woman should wear clothes that accentuate her good points. Simple dresses and gowns, not creations that look like she's going to get up after dinner and sing. . . . The outfit shouldn't compete with the woman. An exception is the overweight woman, where bows, ruffles, and such help distract from the figure.

"Sometimes a star is beautifully costumed on screen but not as tastefully in real life. A famous example was the white halter dress Marilyn Monroe wore in *The Seven Year Itch*. Even when it flared skywards, it emphasized her shapely legs. Travilla designed that, he did an excellent job. . . . A few of the gowns Miss Monroe wore in public were less flattering and more a case of the outfit wearing the woman. . . . We are often called upon to help provide stars with good taste."

—Edith Head, eight-time Oscar-winning costume designer

"The early '60s were an extension of the 1950s. The late '60s differed markedly from the early part of that decade. If Marilyn Monroe had made it into the late 1960s, she'd probably have been a new Marilyn. Still beautiful but not a love goddess. That whole goddess thing sorely hampered her, professionally and personally."

—Christopher Trumbo, writer and son of blacklisted screenwriter Dalton Trumbo

"The dress I remember best isn't necessarily that white one, but the formfitting, flesh-colored one with the sparkly beads Marilyn Monroe wore when she sang 'Happy Birthday' to the president. That was sexy to the max. My guess is it's the reason the president's wife didn't attend that particular birthday celebration."   —E. Lynn Harris, author

"In the 1950s when Hollywood continually emphasized the bust, it occasionally kept you from memorizing the owner's face. . . . Marilyn Monroe, if you want the truth, did not have that large a bust. Had she survived, that would have been fortunate for her; like they say, the bigger they are, the farther they fall. Anyhow, Marilyn's face was a work of art, her best asset, and her bust didn't take away from it."   —Helene Hanff, author

"Marilyn was so inherently feminine that some of her costumers needlessly put her into excessively girlish dresses which gave her a slightly childish aura. I would have given her a more tailored, streamlined look. Even in a man's suit, she would have been alluring. No matter what you'd create for Marilyn, she could never look like a woman in drag. On her, much more than the Mona Lisa, even a mustache would look chic!"
—Bill Blass, fashion designer

"She wore orange—flaming orange—in *Gentlemen Prefer Blondes*. Now, that's a color almost nobody can carry off, and when I heard about it I was livid—'What are they trying to do to poor Marilyn?' Jane Russell, next to Marilyn in that shipboard scene, wears classic black and looks great. That is, if you even look at her. Marilyn is gorgeous, like a glowing, palpitating orange flame, in that dress. How wrong I was!"
—Jack Cole, MM's choreographer

"Marilyn Monroe is only female movie star I have had a crush for. Is like a fantasy, harmless and far away."
                                                              —Rudolf Nureyev

"I worked with all three: Marilyn, Mansfield, and Mamie Van Doren—all sexy ladies who weren't considered exactly ladies, thank goodness. It was a pleasure, even if nothing happened to not write home about. . . . The sexiest of the trio was Marilyn. She had a less forced quality than the others, which is not to put them down, just to tell you my favorite. And the world's."
                                      —Tommy Noonan, costar, *Gentlemen Prefer Blondes*

"It's a cliché now, and maybe Marilyn Monroe originated it: that comment where she's asked does she dress for women or for men, and the slinky answer is, 'I dress for women but undress for men.' It's tough to find out who said something memorable first."
                                                  —Jennifer Beals, actress, *Flashdance*

"With her blonde hair and red lips and dressed in pink or pastels, Marilyn Monroe rather resembled a fun-fair confection."
—Sir Ralph Richardson

"As with most very good-looking movie stars, Marilyn Monroe had an obsession about her looks. In public she liked to look the way she was expected to look, even if it took hours. Joan Crawford, the same thing—and when she stopped looking like Joan Crawford, she became a recluse and stayed in her apartment until she died. My brother, the same— very handsome into his seventies, but then . . . he stayed at home and had very, very few visitors."
                                      —Francisco "Chico" Day, assistant director and brother
                                            of Mexican-born actor Gilbert Roland

"What became her biggest hit was a detriment for Marilyn over the long run. After almost two years since her last picture [*The Prince and the Showgirl*], she chose to go backward. In 1958 she signed to play a character called Sugar Kane [in *Some Like It Hot*] who describes herself as 'just dumb' and is likely alcoholic. At over thirty, another gold-digging showgirl. Marilyn wanted to make time stand still and duplicate her earlier success."   —Eli Wallach, friend and costar, *The Misfits*

"Naturally she thought she was progressing artistically by coming to Britain to do the film of a play by Sir Terence Rattigan, costarring with and directed by Sir Laurence Olivier, for her own company. But the vehicle, au fond, was a piece of fluff. Its storyline . . . it barely had one. Nevertheless when it wasn't a hit, Marilyn must have been devastated.

"She stayed away from filmmaking for a long time, or what was considered a long time for a star not to be working."   —Colin Clark, whose experiences as an assistant on *The Prince and the Showgirl* became the book (and later a movie) *My Week with Marilyn*

"I can see why that English girl [*sic* Michelle Williams] is up for an Academy Award for playing Marilyn Monroe [in *My Week with Marilyn*]. One, it takes guts to take on such a role. Two, she did it about as well as an actress could. But three, no one can play Marilyn Monroe. Who, by the way, didn't have chubby cheeks."

—Skip E. Lowe, Los Angeles cable TV talk-show host

"Sure, she was sexy in *Some Like It Hot*, and it was a crowd-pleasing comedy. But people were laughing at Marilyn as Sugar Kane—even the name's dumb. . . . How much longer could she keep playing types like that? Middle age does arrive and settle upon each and every one of us. Unless of course we die first."   —Keith Andes, costar, *Clash by Night*

"She'd been reluctant to play another dumb blonde in *Some Like It Hot*. One of the excuses [director] Billy Wilder gave Marilyn was that it was historic—set in the Roaring Twenties, when women were supposedly dumber. . . . Marilyn should have been further along in her career than she was. Despite the movie's success it was almost an admission that she couldn't deliver crowds playing anything but the roles—or should I say role—that made her famous."   —Radie Harris, newspaper columnist

"Sure I knew Marilyn. Knew her well. She was wonderful, a wonderful person. . . . Her career and the people in it, most of them, weren't wonderful. Careers in this business end up disappointing the person that has 'em. So it's important to be happy in your real life. Movies aren't real. They're here today and gone tomorrow. I'd rather be here today and gone to Maui."   —Marlon Brando, actor and ex-lover

"I did a scene with Marilyn [in *Something's Got to Give*]. Very beautiful girl. I don't have anything to tell about her and Marlon, who's my best friend. I've teased him that he never got to work with Marilyn. . . . When people are as extremely appealing as they are, everyone wants them and—to be honest—they know it and . . . they're generous people. Not selfish. If I looked like them, I wouldn't be selfish either."   —Wally Cox, actor-comedian

"I don't think there's anything left to say about Marilyn. Though fortunately there's certainly a lot left to dream about her."
—Hugh Hefner, *Playboy* founder

CHAPTER 3

Valentine

"I never disliked Marilyn Monroe or felt in competition with her. . . . As a moviegoer I always felt protective of her character."
—Natalie Wood

"By and large, most people liked Marilyn. It was certain critics, those self-appointed upholders of public morality, who knocked her. As for women moviegoers, she didn't threaten them. Marilyn wasn't worldly, she had an innocence."
—Lauren Bacall, costar, *How to Marry a Millionaire*

"She was great. I didn't get to work with her. . . . You know what else was great about her? The women in the audience liked her too."
—Marlon Brando

"You always rooted for Marilyn. You had to. She was sweet, in addition to anything else. She didn't use men. And in the movies she got cast in, she didn't get used by men the way some other actresses did. . . . It's unfortunate to read that in real life she did apparently get used by men. Plenty."
—Julia Roberts

"There goes the original good time that was had by all."
—Bette Davis (MM had a supporting role in *All About Eve*)

"I was taken to see Raquel Welch's show in Las Vegas. I must say she was spectacular looking. But I didn't like her, and I sensed most of the women didn't either. She came on as arrogant, reveling in her sexuality. The men were drooling, while the women were resentful. . . . She has a pro-men, anti-women vibe mercifully lacking in, for instance, a Marilyn Monroe."   —Joan Didion, writer

"I wasn't surprised when I heard she'd been having an affair with John Kennedy. He was your handsomest and youngest president, and his wife was the most attractive First Lady. So, as in a fairy tale or a Valentine's card, if JFK were to have a girlfriend, it would logically be the most attractive film star. It didn't interfere with his running the country, did it?"   —Coral Browne, British actress

"If it wasn't for Jackie [Kennedy], one would be okay about the Kennedy-Monroe liaison. They look like the perfect couple you'd see atop a wedding cake. But he was married, he was a father, he did have other . . . paramours, and he was in charge of a whole country, after all."   —Merv Griffin, talk-show host

"Our president [François Mitterrand] is widely known to have two mistresses. It is not shocking, only somewhat unusual, since he is older and has two, not one. . . . But the level of taste has declined. Kennedy had Marilyn Monroe. Clinton has Monica [Lewinsky]."   —Gérard Depardieu, French actor

"I think Marilyn saw the romantic-fantasy side of having an affair with a president, while he probably saw her as a trophy lover and not much else. . . . The only thing more remarkable than her thinking she could keep such an affair secret is that the media actually kept it a secret! That could never happen again, for sure."   —Rosie O'Donnell

"When I found out she was having an affair with JFK I thought, Go, girl! But then his brother [Robert Kennedy] was mentioned, and I'm not sure whether she had an affair with him too. If she did, then it gets kind of tacky, like JFK was passing her on down the line. I hope she didn't have an affair with the brother too. That's not the American-princess way I like to think of Marilyn."   —Claudia Schiffer, supermodel

"There were some blonde sex symbols I could name but won't who were easy on the eyes but came across, shall we say, somewhat whorishly. They tried too hard. With Monroe, she didn't seem to be trying at all. She was just naturally, exuberantly sexy. She wasn't selling, she was being herself."   —Phil Donahue, talk-show host

"Marilyn's brand of sexuality wasn't nasty, it was refreshing. . . .
Back then, Americans in particular had so many sexual hang-ups,
that she was bound to be shocking in some quarters."
—Hugh Grant

"The thing about her that could not be said about most actresses whose appeal was sexually based is she wasn't vulgar. Sexy, yes . . . I think the naiveté she performed so well was part of her act. But she wasn't vulgar."
—Gilda Radner, actress-comedian, *Saturday Night Live*

"Well, she has this va-va-voom reputation that precedes her. But when I met and worked with her, I discovered it to be mere publicity. She's a lovely girl, very charming and hardworking. Not a vamp at all." —Cary Grant, costar, *Monkey Business*

"Other gorgeous actresses were also exciting, you followed their lives and their ups and downs . . . like Rita Hayworth or Hedy Lamarr. The difference is, with Marilyn you cared. There was an emotional connection that you didn't have with the other ladies. You felt they could take care of themselves and were maybe, underneath the glitz, rather hard-edged and aloof." —John Frankenheimer, TV and film director

"Fox was very smart in promoting Marilyn Monroe the way they did. They didn't often pair her opposite handsome leading men like Ty Power to present a beautiful couple. They usually put her opposite some nothing-looking ordinary guy . . . that gave the average male moviegoer hope." —Harry Brand, Fox publicity executive

"You notice when Marilyn's male lead was homely or an average Joe, she reacted just as positively toward him as she did when the male lead was a big name or a hunk of man. I think that was really democratic of her!" —Sylvester Stallone

"I have the distinction of having been Miss Monroe's costar more often than any other actor. I can tell you she was a dream of a person, sweet and considerate. . . . I don't know where all this stuff comes from, that she was so difficult and temperamental. Not any more so than any other leading lady or for that matter any top masculine star I've worked with." —David Wayne

"In my book, she rated and will always rate a Valentine. *The Seven Year Itch* was the high point of my long career." –Tom Ewell

"*The Seven Year Itch* included one of the first 'gay' references [regarding two hairdresser neighbors] in any popular American movie. One had to be very cagey about such things then. It was amusing that the character who was being driven to sexual distraction by his neighbor, played by Miss Monroe, was played—and very well too—by a gay actor.

"I know Mr. Ewell would not mind my saying that today, for toward the end of his life he came out of the proverbial closet."

–Billy Wilder, the film's cowriter-director

"Marilyn's affairs and marriages never lasted very long. Some of her friendships did, but the relationship she hoped would be for a lifetime was if she had a child. She might have put up with the disappointing second or third marriage if either had produced offspring."

–Ralph Roberts, masseur and friend

"When Marilyn became involved with Joe DiMaggio, it was advertised as the most romantic pairing possible. Then we found out things about his temper. . . . When she linked up with Arthur Miller, that was another relationship [that] turned out to be not that happy behind the scenes.

"It's revealing about us, not her, that we insist on Marilyn Monroe as an icon of romance and joy, even though we know her relationships were far from ideal, and none of them lasted."

–Dr. Margaret Mead, anthropologist

"It's interesting that she didn't get romantically close to any Hollywood actor. At some point, most actresses become intimate with an actor or other man in the business. For whatever reason, Marilyn seemed to avoid them."

—Donald O'Connor, costar, *There's No Business Like Show Business*

"Marilyn Monroe was ambitious, but her way. From day one in Hollywood, she could have gone on endless studio-arranged dates with famous actors, including gay ones. But instead of seeking publicity as half a pair, she was posing on her own and studying and networking, keeping busy behind and in front of the scenes."

—Joyce Haber, *Los Angeles Times* columnist

"Girls ask me all the time how they can be like Marilyn Monroe, and I tell them if they showed one-tenth of the hard work and gumption that that girl had, they'd be on their way."

—Emmeline Snively, Blue Book Modeling Agency owner-manager who gave MM her first modeling job in 1945

"Marilyn is quite a product of our generation, and it would be an honor for any girl to be able to emulate her."

—Joanne Woodward

"She knows the world, but this knowledge has not lowered her great and benevolent dignity. . . . Its darkness has not dimmed her goodness."

—Dame Edith Sitwell, British poet and critic

"A lot of people will tell you it's all publicity. That's malarkey. They've tried to give a hundred girls the same publicity buildup. It didn't take with them."

—Joseph Cotten on his *Niagara* costar

"She was extra photogenic and enjoyed being photographed. Most people do not enjoy the process. It usually shows if they don't. They unknowingly create a barrier between themselves and the camera so that you don't see the real person, the natural individual. Marilyn had no such barrier, and she was very willing, able, and athletic. She told me she'd do whatever I wanted—cartwheels, handstands, climb a tree. . . . I photographed her doing all of those. She did a superior cartwheel!" —Earl Leaf, photographer

"Relaxation is crucial to good acting. Inhibitions put a wall between an actor and the viewer. Actresses tend to be less inhibited than actors . . . too many actors seem emotionally constipated. . . . Two of the most naturally free actresses I can think of are Marilyn Monroe and Meryl Streep." —Peggy Feury, acting coach

"She usually draped herself in a towel. If it slid off, okay.
She didn't care if she had anything on or not, and this was
before nudity was in. She was ahead of her time."
—stylist George Masters on doing MM's hair

"Marilyn was very accepting of the whole human condition. As I have often said, nothing human disgusts me except unkindness, a philosophy which she shared. Unlike most people born in her generation, she didn't think sex was dirty. She didn't carry a sense of guilt. She would only be ashamed if sex were forced." —Tennessee Williams

"She knew what the realities of the times were, but Marilyn was against the closet. What she told me about Montgomery Clift is becoming sort of famous. She said that people who weren't fit to open the door for him would ridicule his homosexuality and that she laughed about rumors that she was lesbian. Her conclusion was 'No sex is wrong if there's love in it.' Marilyn was ahead of her time."   —W. J. Weatherby, journalist

"It's ironic that in spite of Elizabeth Taylor's father being gay, she was aloof to Marilyn Monroe not just because of professional rivalry, but the gossip that Marilyn went both ways. Not that Taylor was homophobic—so long as the gay individual was male."
—Gore Vidal

"It's so incongruous. She was this blonde, updated Betty Boop figure as well as somebody the FBI kept an ever-growing file on since 1955. The last I've heard [in 1999], it's still heavily censored for 'security reasons.'"   —Pauline Kael, film critic

"I used to fantasize about what if I could go back in time and date Marilyn Monroe. But I understand she almost never dated actors. At least she liked Jewish guys."
—Jerry Seinfeld

"Liz wasn't too happy when Marilyn and Monty bonded during *The Misfits*. I don't know how that played itself out, but Monty was Liz's best bud. Although it was platonic between him and Marilyn, Liz was somewhat intimidated by her beauty. Liz has her own insecurities; she'll say Ava Gardner is her idea of a really beautiful woman. Conversely, as an actress Liz looked down on Marilyn and felt no competition there."   —Taylor pal Rock Hudson

"Marilyn was pro-Jewish, pro-black, pro-gay, you name it, before it was acceptable. J. Edgar Hoover [the FBI director], who was somewhere to the right of Attila the Hun, hated all that, and he hated Marilyn.

"When she heard that a nightclub in Los Angeles wouldn't hire Ella Fitzgerald because she was black, Marilyn told the owners if they booked Ella she'd sit at a front table every night. They did and she did, and it was big-time publicity for Ella, who said she never had to sing in another tiny venue, thanks to Marilyn."
—Shari Lewis, ventriloquist and author who was Jewish

"It doesn't get publicized, but one of the most daring things Marilyn did, in an age when women weren't supposed to be interested in the world beyond their kitchen and boudoir, was to sponsor the National Committee for a Sane Nuclear Policy. That does merit mention."
—Martin Sheen

"Marilyn was seduced by Yves Montand and his Gallic charm during *Let's Make Love*. She thought him romantic. For him, she was the biggest notch on his belt. When she started to get serious, he dropped her, then told the press back home that the aggressive American star had thrown herself at him!"   —George Cukor, the film's director

"I was not happy about it, but our marriage survived. And if he had to have his Hollywood 'fling,' why not with Marilyn Monroe? I can understand that."
—Simone Signoret, French actress whose marriage to
Yves Montand lasted until Signoret's death

"She walked down the aisle three times and found out that romance usually ends after the honeymoon does. Marilyn was a born romantic. But I'm not sure if she'd lived [that] she'd have married again. The first marriage was a blue-collar situation, but the next two left psychological scars." —Barbara Stanwyck, costar, *Clash by Night*

"We worked together in *Don't Bother to Knock*, early in our careers.
Although we didn't really have any scenes together, we did meet.
She was concerned about her part. . . . This wasn't a romantic comedy,
and she played a very neurotic girl. But she sincerely reached out to me,
and we were each happy for the other's professional success. That was
not too common among actresses back in the '50s."
—Anne Bancroft

"It was the biggest break I've ever had, and she was more beautiful than anyone I ever saw in my life. She was real nice to me, really sweet, and I was just a kid, but she made me feel like a teenager. . . . Like so many people who met her, I used to wonder if we'd stayed in touch could I somehow have made a difference in her life, could I have helped her live longer?

"In my memory, she's like an angel."   —George "Foghorn" Winslow, costar
(as young Henry Spofford III), *Gentlemen Prefer Blondes*

"The secret of acting is listening. In acting for the camera, as opposed to the stage,
you speak softly and listen loudly. Marilyn knew this instinctively, and it's why she's so convincing as well as so empathic in her films."
—Montgomery Clift, friend and costar, *The Misfits*

"Clint modeled his breathy voice on Marilyn Monroe, figuring audiences would listen more closely than if he were loud."

—Sondra Locke, Eastwood's ex-girlfriend, costar, and biographer

"Marilyn was a great listener . . . a good shoulder for someone to cry on. She cared, not just superficially. But whether she in turn was given much empathy . . . She needed a reliable shoulder, and no one man provided that."

—Lena Pepitone, employee and biographer of MM

"Marilyn craved people's approval, which may have come from a deprived childhood. She was especially tenderhearted toward children and animals. Her feeling for the doomed horses in *The Misfits* comes across powerfully, and if she were alive today, I'm in no doubt that she would be active for animals' rights."

—Betty White

"I remember Marilyn saying that she liked books but she also liked people. She grew to love reading, but she also enjoyed being part of a group or family. . . . She didn't enjoy being on a movie set—she usually felt she was there as the main attraction or a freak show, certainly not part of a family."

—Susan Strasberg, friend and actress

"Between a good-looking guy and a smart one, Marilyn would always choose the smart one. Looks, she already had. More smarts, well, who couldn't use some more?"

—Shelley Winters, actress and one-time roommate

"Marilyn wasn't one of those stars who always needs to be the center of attention. She had enough of that when she went out of doors. In regular life, she preferred being one of a group. She wanted acceptance." —Jack Cole, friend and choreographer

"The way I heard it, when Arthur Miller was dating Marilyn Monroe, he took her to his parents' home three nights in a row, and each night his mother served them soup with matzo balls. Finally, Marilyn whispered to Arthur, 'Don't Jewish people ever use any other part of the poor matzo?'" —Alan King, comedian

"There were some mean-spirited newspaper columnists like Hedda Hopper and Mike Connolly who, when Marilyn had trouble doing a scene and getting a line of dialogue right in the first few takes, they reported it—trying to make her look incompetent instead of nervous. Why report it at all?" —Theresa Russell, who played MM in the film *Insignificance*

"The studios and the press have long identified being blond with being unintelligent or untalented. I had to suffer through that for much of my career. . . . I've been labeled 'the male Marilyn Monroe.' But I never saw her called 'the female Troy Donahue.'" —Troy Donahue

"Sidney Skolsky the famous columnist became an ally to Marilyn Monroe and helped push her up the ladder as America's Sweetheart. However, he thought the way to do that was to present her as a dumb bunny. . . . Initially, she went along with that." —Betty Friedan, feminist and author, *The Feminine Mystique*

"She was a supporter of the civil rights movement, but she was hemmed in by her studio and career. . . . She already had enemies without opening her mouth, let alone being political."

—Lena Horne

"Marilyn would come up with clever answers to potential interview questions. For instance, when asked about the famous nude pose, she quipped, 'It's not true that I had nothing on. I had the radio on.'"   —Max Showalter, costar, *Niagara*

"In Britain we had English Roses, who were lovely and ladylike but not sex symbols. There were some exceptions, starting in the 1950s and '60s. One was Caroline Munro, a buxom brunette whose name was meant to sound like Marilyn Monroe. She was cast in a 007 picture and had a flourishing career here."

—Ronald Neame, director, *The Prime of Miss Jean Brodie*

"I was billed as 'Britain's Answer to Marilyn Monroe,' but I came on stronger . . . perhaps that's why I didn't make much of a dent in the American market. They preferred demure and soft-spoken blondes, while I often played sexual aggressors.

"In due time my career as well as my assets began to sag, but it was fun while it lasted, and I think I've enjoyed it more than Marilyn did."   —Diana Dors (neé Diana Fluck)

"It's breaking my heart. . . . Marilyn's costume from *Bus Stop* is only one of the irreplaceable pieces of Hollywood history that will be up for sale."

—Debbie Reynolds on the 2010 foreclosure auction of her memorabilia collection, which was intended as the basis of a Hollywood museum

"Marilyn paid the price of authenticity with her characteristic cocktail of grace, forbearance, and grief. She strove for an elusive admixture of hope and industry, will and willingness until her final days. She possessed an able, grownup-lady femininity that now more than ever is in too short supply."

—Lisa Rosman, writer, *Los Angeles Weekly*, in 2010

"Most fans stayed in love with Marilyn Monroe as she matured. But her final roles didn't keep up with her. Times were changing . . . 'sex kittens' like Ann-Margret were wilder and more independent. Who knows how much longer Marilyn would have remained big box office?
"Mary Pickford was for a long while America's valentine. But she played those girlish characters too often and fell out of favor for being older than her roles."

—Dr. Ruth Westheimer, sexologist

"I was informed that after she saw herself in the bikini in *The Misfits*, Miss Monroe was unhappy because she had gained some weight and her tummy pooched out. . . . In those days girls didn't have to be as slim as now [the 1970s], and men often did—and do—like rounded surfaces.

"But with the 1960s the desired silhouette was more boyish. Tummies were out [they were] supposed to be flat. By the filming of her next and final [uncompleted] film, she had thinned her face and figure and, in my opinion, looked her very best since 1953 and her signature films *Gentlemen Prefer Blondes* and *How to Marry a Millionaire*."

—Cristóbal Balenciaga, couturier

"The pendulum swings. In the late '50s and early '60s Monroe was replaced as the movies' favorite blonde by Doris Day. Besides musicals and the occasional drama, the versatile Day did sex comedies while playing the eternal virgin . . . and became World Film Favorite [Golden Globe] for five years in a row. After Marilyn died, her incomplete movie (*Something's Got to Give*) was retooled as a Doris Day vehicle (*Move Over, Darling*)."
—Ken Ferguson, editor of UK *Photoplay*

"Doris Day was criticized as 'the eternal virgin,' and Marilyn Monroe as her opposite, yet she wasn't. Look, for example, at *The Seven Year Itch* or *The Prince and the Showgirl*. In each, the man tries to seduce her but does not. Marilyn never goes to bed with him and never reveals a soupçon of nudity. Neither deserved so much, how do you say, opprobrium. Sometimes from people who never even saw their movies."
—François Truffaut, film critic turned director

"There's more to people than their looks. The proof is models, female or male. Some look stunning, then you meet them and, like, nobody's home. There's nothing beyond the physical architecture. Gorgeous but no sex appeal. Other people can be less than physically ideal and just ooze sex appeal.

"If Marilyn Monroe had looked the way she did but had nothing more than that ideal facade, she wouldn't have become the star and the beloved icon she became. And people wouldn't feel about her the way they still do."
—Roseanne

"There's a more multilayered perception of Marilyn Monroe today. We go beyond the surface. Time and the feminist movement have given us more understanding. In the Eisenhower era, she was perceived more as a sensation than a real performer, and most people, men in particular, saw only blonde hair and sex . . . maybe somebody to laugh at or take advantage of. There wasn't that much humanity in most men's perception of Marilyn Monroe."   —Tom Ammiano, comedian turned San Francisco politician

"Joe DiMaggio slugged her . . . more than once. Now we know about it. Back then, known or not, it wouldn't have been reported. Worse, it wouldn't even have been condemned by most people. There weren't any words for sexual harassment or wife battering . . . almost no laws against it. It was deemed part of everyday life . . . and still going on in the '60s when George C. Scott was having an affair with Ava Gardner and slugged her during filming [of *The Bible*].

"The ones who knew and sometimes told—but not to the media—were the makeup people."   —Janet Charlton, columnist

"The longer Marilyn Monroe has been dead, the brighter the halo she now wears. The image of promiscuity that she was saddled with is now very faded. Of course, it was always exaggerated. Scandal mongers in and away from Hollywood claimed Marilyn was having affairs with almost every man she met, and a few women as well. Had she had half the affairs they claimed, she would never have had the time to appear in nearly thirty motion pictures."
—Arthur Marx, author and son of Groucho

"I couldn't believe [Elizabeth Hurley's] remarks about Marilyn Monroe being fat, and how Liz Hurley would sooner drop dead than look like that. As a model Liz has worked on her body. . . . I think now it's time for her to work on her personality."

—fellow Brit Boy George

"Hollywood is filled with men who brag that they had an affair with Marilyn Monroe . . . also with parties who declare they discovered her or lent her money for a makeover or to buy clothes or what have you. Most anyone who met her remembers her vividly. Alas, many who 'remember' her never met her."
—Donald O'Connor, costar,
There's No Business Like Show Business

"I was watching the Mike Douglas talk show, and one guest was an elderly gossip columnist [James Bacon]. Out of nowhere he announces that he slept with Marilyn Monroe. I started to become angry, but I didn't have to, because another guest, that English actor Oliver Reed, told him off and said he had no business saying that publicly, true or not . . . that he was defaming and cheapening a lady who was no longer there to defend herself."

—Eileen Heckart, costar, *Bus Stop*

"Anyone who claims a more than passing or costarring relationship with Marilyn Monroe, I'd ask them for proof. I know it's not usually available, but with someone as giant as Marilyn, with such a huge legacy, you have to take anything you hear with a grain of salt. Or twenty grains."

—Jennifer Lopez

"Marilyn learned her craft and developed her talent. Unlike so many today, she earned her fame. She didn't become famous via bad behavior like a Britney Spears or via a brand name, like a Paris Hilton. She didn't get publicity with tantrums, like a Shannen Doherty, or become a purported sex symbol like Anna Nicole Smith via opportunism and marrying an antique billionaire. Marilyn puts today's no-talents and bad girls to shame."

—Helmut Newton, photographer

"Interestingly, Marilyn stayed closer to her husband's relatives than to the two men. She stayed buddies with Joe DiMaggio Jr. and with Arthur Miller's father. After the divorces, she wrote letters and telephoned regularly. She didn't like to give up a friendship. Or a family, which is what she valued most."

—David Shaw, TV writer

"For all the emphasis on sex in her image and publicity, for Marilyn the f-word meant family. She wanted to belong. When there was a platonic man in her life, like a psychiatrist or writer friend, she'd want to meet and become friends with his wife and kids and feel welcome in their home. . . . She never really got any family of her own."
—Dr. Michael M. Gurdin, friend

"All her life she lived in other people's houses or in apartments. Not until the last nine months of her life did she finally own her own home. She was so excited about that. But just nine months . . ."

—Suzy Parker, model turned actress

"Marilyn craved continuity. When you grow up in several different homes, continuity is a luxury, and you crave stability. It's chancy enough for civilians to secure a continuing marriage, but heaven help the rich and famous."   —Jack Cole, friend and choreographer

"She was clearly more at ease with the very young—children—and with old people. They liked her for herself. . . . With grown male heterosexuals she'd know they wanted either or both of two things from her: sex or advancement. And with grown homosexual men, most would still seek advancement. Very few people weren't out to try and get something from Marilyn Monroe."   —Kurt Goldstein, neurologist-psychiatrist

"After her late twenties or so, Marilyn liked the idea of marrying a man who was a father, so she could marry into a ready-made family."
—Shelley Winters, actress and one-time roommate

"They have one big park in L.A. [Griffith Park], and apparently it's almost out of town. Marilyn loved nature and walking, which she often did once she moved to Manhattan. . . . She told a friend of mine that an advantage of walking, versus driving all the time like in L.A., is one might meet a nice man that way, especially in a nice neighborhood. Makes sense."   —Robert Whitehead, theater producer, Broadway's *Bus Stop*

"We wanted Marilyn to stay. We didn't want her to go back to Los Angeles. She brought excitement and glamour to New York, and if she'd stayed with us she might have had a longer and, to be honest, a better-quality career. Not to mention hopefully a longer life."
—Maureen Stapleton, stage actress

"Marilyn Monroe got top billing in *Some Like It Hot*, but it centered around Tony Curtis and Jack Lemmon. Lemmon stole the show because though he and Curtis did drag—and Curtis made a better-looking woman—Jack just ran with it. He found the joy in the role. Curtis didn't. Jack made his Daphne into a whole other character, a madcap delight who audiences loved. Tony and Marilyn weren't thrilled about that."

—Penelope Fitzgerald, British author

"When Tony made that awful comment about kissing her being like kissing Hitler, Marilyn told the papers, 'That's his problem.' But it wounded her deeply. She couldn't understand why he said it, and it made her doubt her own appeal to him. They'd actually dated when they were rising stars. . . . Could be the comment was Tony's way of getting back at Marilyn for her tardiness. Or he resented her being billed over him or maybe he had secret Nazi fantasies. Whoever knows?"
—Janet Leigh, Curtis's ex-wife and actress, *Psycho*

"I got along fine with Marilyn. Tony had more scenes with her, so he had to wait for her more often than I did. . . . I came to see that her lack of punctuality wasn't a power trip or at all about laziness. Marilyn had to feel ready for the camera . . . she had to psych herself up, and that could take time.

"I'd get upset myself, now and then. But I couldn't stay upset. She was a dear . . . as well as the fact that here she was, struggling to stay on top, and if there's one thing more difficult than making it to the top, it's staying up there."

—Jack Lemmon, costar, *Some Like It Hot*

"When she apologized for being late, it was real. I've seen stars show up late and act like we should be grateful they showed up at all—that is, if their last movie was a hit. Or else they show up and mumble a fraction of an apology—if their last movie was a flop."

—Hope Lange, costar, *Bus Stop*

"New York actors can be frank to the point of rudeness. But then some go to Hollywood and become deceitful and rude. Like a friend of mine's ex-boyfriend who used to be called Bernie Schwartz."   —actress and friend Susan Strasberg, talking about Tony Curtis

"Among star actresses, a sizeable percentage are quite aware of their ability to turn men on . . . [and] some use it like a weapon or at least a calling card. With Marilyn, when I met and spoke to her, she seemed completely unaware of her looks. We were simply two people talking, communicating."

—James Mason

"Marilyn liked the camaraderie of fellow actors. . . . She wanted to please. Most superstars don't care if they please—unless it's pleasing themselves. Incidentally, I find that word utterly misleading. The only superstar with which I am acquainted is the sun."

—Elsa Lanchester, actress, *The Bride of Frankenstein*

"Stardom changed Marilyn Monroe less than most stars. She seemed to keep her good human qualities while also keeping her bad habits of ignoring the clock and not gaining confidence. . . . I would alternate between feeling sorry for her and mad at her. But when she did show up, suddenly the wait was worth it!" —Tony Randall, costar, *Let's Make Love*

"If anyone met Marilyn Monroe and told somebody else, the first question would always be, 'What does she look like?' Even though everyone knew what she looked like. The subtext was: Does she still look good? Are her looks going?"

—Lauren Bacall, costar, *How to Marry a Millionaire*

"An actor doesn't have to spend anywhere as much time preparing with costume and makeup and hairstyling as an actress. When I was in *El Cid*, I often heard how angry Charlton Heston was because he thought it was my fault he was waiting. But I couldn't have gotten away if I wanted to! Everyone was working on how I looked. . . . I imagine the same thing happened to Marilyn Monroe, but more often—and also because of touching up blonde hair, that also takes time."

—Sophia Loren

"It's not difficult to puzzle out. In those days an actress of thirty or more was considered over the hill. Marilyn Monroe turned thirty in 1956, and she got to the set later and later. It took her more and more time to 'look like Marilyn Monroe.' She didn't wish to disappoint people."

—Germaine Greer, Australian feminist and author, *The Female Eunuch*

"Marilyn liked women and prized her female friendships. But she didn't have many within the business. The majority of other actresses, older as well as younger, were hoping Marilyn's beauty would wither. This is an ultracompetitive business, and often a mean one."

—Susan Strasberg, actress and friend

"It's ironic that while millions of men would have given their eyeteeth to go on a date with Marilyn Monroe, there were lots of Saturday nights when she was in alone and lonely."

—James Bacon, columnist

"Marilyn was a little too concerned with being liked. She could have handled some of the dramatic things that went Kim Novak's way. Novak was in the same general niche. But Marilyn didn't want to play a character the audience would hate. She once said that she envied Mary Pickford's nickname of America's Sweetheart. They were still calling Pickford that long after she'd retired, which Marilyn thought was splendid."

—Peter Hunt, British director, *On Her Majesty's Secret Service*

"On screen, Marilyn didn't mind standing up to a man. But she avoided playing out-and-out seductresses, which she found demeaning, or women who treat men in a demeaning way. . . . About the last type of role she'd have played would be Martha in *Who's Afraid of Virginia Woolf?*" —Richard Barr, stage producer, *Who's Afraid of Virginia Woolf?*

"Elizabeth was jealous of Marilyn . . . she thought she got by too easily, on her looks. Marilyn envied Liz getting the meatier roles. Especially *Cleopatra*, which was a part Marilyn would never get, since Cleopatra was of Greek origin and Marilyn wouldn't dye her hair. Besides, she might not have had the regal authority to portray, in essence, a dictator."
—Roddy McDowall

"Despite her sexy image and the blondes-have-more-fun stereotype, I believe Marilyn spent more time with books than with men. Books could benefit her . . . most men, not so much. More than a few of her sincere friends were old fuddie-duddies like myself."

—Norman Rosten, writer

CHAPTER 4

Venus

"The Greeks had Aphrodite, the goddess of love and beauty. The Romans called her Venus. The modern world has Marilyn . . . and if you have to ask, Marilyn who? [then] you're not part of the modern world."

—Dr. Phil

"Golden-age Hollywood had a few genuine goddesses . . . Garbo and Dietrich. No American ones. Not till Marilyn Monroe died."

—Dorothy Arzner, director

"Rome's emperors were made into gods whom its citizens were forced to worship. Modern people may choose to worship Marilyn."

—William A. Zanghi, Italian-American professor

"I think in her day, Marilyn Monroe was only lusted after. Now, she's loved. There's a big difference. I think this is what she wanted all along."
—Meryl Streep

"Every woman who goes blonde wants to look like Marilyn Monroe. The sad truth is, they can't. On the other hand, almost no woman wants to be Marilyn—not with the sad life and tragic end she had."

—Gwyneth Paltrow

"When the media started comparing me to Marilyn Monroe, I was as flattered as if they'd complimented my singing. Which was sort of foolish on my part, if you analyze it."

—singer Deborah Harry of Blondie

"I've read that the two most charismatic stars ever were Garbo and Marilyn. I admire both, but it must be said that Garbo often struck poses. She's stunning, but she does seem old-fashioned now. I think Marilyn will always be thoroughly contemporary."

—Raquel Welch, the first major post-MM sex symbol

"There are two aspects to Marilyn that we see and appreciate today. The beauty, of course, accompanied by her unique personality. But also the lesson that this woman, during a time when women were undervalued, was a tragic victim. She is at once an inspiration and a warning."

—Dr. Betty Berzon, psychologist and author

"Growing up, I liked so many fantastic actresses. Marilyn Monroe was one of the tops. Many of us girls had crushes on her. Many of us wanted to look like her. But that's impossible. Even so, we didn't hate her for it. I don't think anyone could hate her."

—Angelina Jolie

"In the 1950s the two biggest actresses were Marilyn Monroe and Audrey Hepburn. Each wonderful in her own way. They were the two feminine ideals, and millions of females wanted to look like them. But let's be honest, it was more practical to try and look like Audrey than Marilyn Monroe."

—Maria Callas, opera diva

"Maria was fat, so she decided to diet. She wanted a body that didn't contradict her beautiful voice. Her favorite cinema stars were Audrey Hepburn and Marilyn Monroe. Maria didn't want to dye her hair, and it's almost impossible to achieve the Monroe figure if you don't have the prerequisites, so she placed a photo of Hepburn on her refrigerator and dieted very successfully.

"When someone wrote in the newspapers that Maria resembled Audrey Hepburn, she was in seventh heaven. For the rest of her life, she kept the extra weight off."
—Jackie Kalogeropoulos, Maria Callas's sister

"We got a wonderful reaction to my [Marilyn] imitation on *I Love Lucy*. People wrote in and asked for more. . . . Some executive or other suggested we do a whole episode around it, but I said no. I'd done it once, briefly, it was fun, and maybe I did a good job, but that was it. I'm no Marilyn Monroe."
—Lucille Ball

"There's this Marilyn imitator called, I think, Jimmy James. In photos he and one other imitator who I don't remember, resemble her, ironically, more than any females I've seen. . . . You know how some female impersonators make careers out of 'being' Streisand or Bette Davis or Cher? No guy's been able to make a career out of Marilyn. It's like she's off-limits. The ultimate feminine . . . which no man can ape."
—Helmut Newton, photographer

"The Muppet people did a poster of Miss Piggy imitating Marilyn Monroe in her white upswept dress that was hilarious. It lampooned the futility of trying to re-create a one-of-a-kind classic."
—Dr. Joyce Brothers, psychologist

"You can see what Marilyn Monroe had that others don't when they make movies about her or copy the famous white dress flying up past her legs. Because whatever actress plays her in that dress or poses for a still-camera recreation simply doesn't compare."
—Walter Bernstein, screenwriter, *Something's Got to Give*

"That is the most famous dress ever made. Think about it.
Can you even name another famous dress or gown? And her pose,
standing over that Manhattan subway grating, the wind blowing the
skirt of her dress up over her beautiful bare legs, with a glimpse of
white panties, it's iconic. It's been imitated umpteen times,
never successfully. The original reigns supreme."
—Jerry Seinfeld

"It defies the tenets of decency of our religion to use such an outrageous image to sell an American-style food to our people."
—commentator Mesut Ozkok on Turkish TV in 2010, talking about a billboard ad for fried chicken featuring a hen's head over Marilyn Monroe's body in the white upswept dress, with the tagline "We Have the Best Legs"
(A similar ad appeared in Mexico a few years earlier.)

"Here in Japan, Ms. Monroe's record albums sell very popularly. She recorded many songs in her career, and the record collections of her singing are purchased by people of all ages, including many who were born after she worked and died."
—*The Best of Marilyn Monroe* liner notes (purchased by this writer in Kyoto in May 1982)

"Miss Marilyn Monroe is even today [2007] the advertising face for several products worldwide, legally or otherwise. This is less an attempt to capitalize on her renowned image of popularity than acknowledgment that she is beyond time and nationality and people stop to pay attention when they see her." —Howard Oladapo, Nigerian columnist

"I guess you have to die to be really appreciated. Marilyn got her share of flak when she was alive. What she'd make of all this adulation and the commercialism, I don't know. But I think she'd be pretty thrilled." —Jane Russell, costar, *Gentlemen Prefer Blondes*

"She was a very healthy girl when she came on the scene, physically and mentally. . . . People picked on her, she was terribly abused for no reason. She became sick—and posthumously they gave her acclaim." —Ann-Margret

"If she'd gotten only one-fourth of the love and esteem she now gets, after she's no longer here to experience it, Marilyn would still be alive today." —Susan Strasberg, actress, friend, and biographer

"I keep hearing about the unhappy Marilyn, over and over, and I say b.s. I didn't know that Marilyn. I didn't know the lady all that well, but all the times I met her or ran into her, she was smiling and happy. She loved being a movie star. Hell, she worked hard for it! Maybe she was unhappy when she was all alone, or maybe she was a better actress than we ever gave her credit for." —Dean Martin

"I think what happens is a collective guilt. On the order of 'We didn't treat them well while they were alive, let's make up for it posthumously.' Like with Marilyn or James Dean. We turn them into superhuman figures of tragic destiny and we stop seeing them as human beings. We forget we ever criticized them or took them for granted. We act as if we always loved Marilyn, because we had great taste."   —Pauline Kael, film critic

"Well, there's a human tendency to change our view of people who died young into a tearful one. We develop a sort of cult, even a religion [and] leave out the laughter and foibles. . . . We turn them into images, icons, posters, surfaces. Like Marilyn—she's a beautiful surface. That's what sells, what people seem to prefer." —Robert Wise, director

"Everyone's seen cards and posters and covers and photos of Marilyn Monroe, and people buy up these things—the proof is, manufacturers keep making them. But you'd be surprised how many people have never seen her in a movie, although videos of Monroe's movies sell consistently and quite well."
          —Richard Condon, film publicist and author of, *Prizzi's Honor*

"I did several quality films with Orson Welles. I did one picture with Miss Monroe. Yet interviewers for more decades than I care to count will ask me ten questions about Marilyn Monroe to every question I get about Orson."
          —Joseph Cotten, costar, *Niagara*

"I find it interesting as well as gratifying that the two most celebrated movie actresses and sex symbols of my era, Marilyn Monroe and Elizabeth Taylor, converted to Judaism and, even after their divorces, remained Jewish."   —Piper Laurie (née Rosetta Jacobs), actress

"If Marilyn had become a mother, how would that have changed her or her image? I can guess about one thing: She was raised Christian and became Jewish, but I think she'd have been and urged her child toward Buddhism. It fit her the best—the gentlest, most philosophic, and realistic. Einstein himself said if he wasn't Jewish he'd be Buddhist."

—Shelley Winters, actress and one-time roommate

"What if Marilyn Monroe had lived? . . . That's the big question for me. Not 'To be or not to be.'"

—British (male) singer Marilyn

"She couldn't know what a sensational career move that was, to go and die young."

—(male) singer Marilyn Manson

"You could envy Marilyn Monroe about dying when she did. Not having to experience aging and see it on yourself, and have others see it. Then you sit down and think more deeply, and there's nothing wrong with aging. It means surviving. A really long life, so long as you're healthy and sound of mind, is the quintessential and normal human goal."

—Peter Sarsgaard, actor, *Dead Man Walking*

"Did she or didn't she? Seems like so many movie stars have tried to kill themselves, but when they finally do die, like Marilyn or Judy, you wonder was it on purpose or was it just an accident?"

—Peter Allen, Australian singer-songwriter who was briefly Judy Garland's son-in-law

"Where drugs and overdoses are concerned, it's usually a matter of time. But I think if Marilyn Monroe would have killed herself, it would have been around the time of one of her three miscarriages, and not in the summer of 1962, when she was battling for her career."
—Jean Peters, costar, *Niagara*

"What they don't often let you know—I don't know why—is that after Twentieth Century Fox fired Marilyn from *Something's Got to Give*, she got them to rehire her. The studio hired her back! Why isn't that made known in those documentaries?"
—John Hughes, director

"I don't buy it at all. Marilyn was not suicidal, and the reason I know is that the same year, 1962, she bought her very first house. That house over on Helena Drive was her first home, her very own. She was very proud of it and of finally being an owner. She was bursting with ideas for furnishing and decorating it."
—Roddy McDowall, actor and photographer

"Marilyn was still decorating her new house when she died. She loved doing that. She was so busy that summer, between the new place and the movie, the nearly-nude photos that kicked Liz Taylor off the magazine covers, then the firing, her campaign to get rehired and generate positive publicity, then getting hired again. . . .

"I think ending it all was the last thing on Marilyn's mind, and she was really trying to kick those prescription drugs, which unfortunately she would mix with champagne."
—Wally Cox, costar, *Something's Got to Give*

"It took time for the Kennedy connection to be revealed to the public, but then it fueled endless conspiracy theories about Marilyn Monroe's death. That either they'd caused it or, more often, that it was done by someone who hated the Kennedys, to embarrass them. Such as J. Edgar Hoover at the FBI. He later smeared Jean Seberg, the American actress living in France . . . said she'd had a baby by a Black Panther. Her lover had been Hispanic—she even showed the baby to the press. But soon afterward she took her own life."
                                        —Joyce Haber, *Los Angeles Times* columnist

"I think there used to be more speculation about what caused Marilyn's death. Now the focus is more on her life and work and what she brought to others. I think that's healthier. Being preoccupied with someone's death and how they died seems morbid and useless. It's what Marilyn did in the time that she had that counts."
—Janet Jackson

"Any large and rich family, there's bound to be dirt. The thing I wonder whenever there's dirt about the Kennedys is, who's behind it? Is it someone anti-Democrat? When I hear that JFK may have been responsible for Marilyn Monroe's death, or his brother Bobby may have been, I question the source. Where's the proof? Is there any whatsoever?

"The media loves linking big names. Their glamour and power somehow make it less important to get the evidence to support the fanciful theories linking those names."
                                        —Ruth Batchelor, TV broadcaster

"If anyone thinks less of Marilyn Monroe because she had an affair with a married man, I'd like to know if they think less of the male politician for having an affair when he's married? Besides, showbiz and politics have always made secret bedfellows—and sometimes they both are fellows."　　　　　　　—Barton Mumaw, dancer-choreographer

"First, you heard that she had an affair with John F. Kennedy. Then with Robert F. Kennedy. I'm surprised they haven't involved Teddy [Kennedy]. . . . We now know JFK was rampantly promiscuous—and I'm leaving out adulterous. Marilyn was a movie star and single. I'm not that disappointed in her. But he was the president, his duty was our country. I am disappointed in him."　　　—Kim Hunter, actress, *A Streetcar Named Desire*

"On one of those cable TV shows about the life and death of Marilyn Monroe, this irritating male voice said that she wanted to become America's First Lady. Did you ever? Didn't this guy know Kennedy already had a wife, and no president had ever been divorced and Marilyn couldn't possibly have been so dumb to think she'd ever be First Lady? Sometimes you just have to laugh at cable TV."
—Uma Thurman

"I read Marilyn Monroe once had lunch with Bobby Kennedy. From that, the media comes up with an entire relationship—sexual, of course. Not that it couldn't have happened. But like with [J. Edgar] Hoover. He wore drag to one Halloween party, so then he's a lifelong cross-dresser. Or when I went out with my sister for dinner, and some tabloid TV program shows the clip and says there I am with my new girlfriend—she's my sister! Where's the *facts*, man?!"　　　　　　　　—Antonio Sabato Jr.

"Some people say Marilyn was killed because she was going to reveal that she'd been having an affair with JFK. Or RFK. Why on earth would she want to do that? Or is it that some people don't think a woman can keep a secret? Angie Dickinson—and everybody knows this—had an affair with JFK. I mean, who didn't? Angie hasn't told about it, and she's over sixty now."

—Jean Howard, party hostess and author, *Jean Howard's Hollywood: A Photo Memoir*

"I do not condemn Mademoiselle Monroe. She is a good customer."
—Gabrielle "Coco" Chanel, fashion designer whose perfume sales were boosted when MM declared Chanel No. 5 her favorite perfume

"When Dior said the New Look had no bust, I don't think Hollywood paid much attention. Even the French decided to model their postwar ideal on such love goddesses as Marilyn Monroe, Brigitte Bardot, and the Venus de Milo, the goddess of love."

—Kay Thompson, singer-actress

"Most of the time when you see Marilyn posthumously, it's photos she posed for rather than stills from her movies. She began as a pinup and model, though not a high-fashion model. She was too sexy for that. Haute couture required cool, aloof women. Thank goodness Marilyn was a tireless poser. She enjoyed it, and we can still enjoy seeing her enjoying herself."

—Kim Basinger

"Why do we like to look at Marilyn Monroe? Because we like to look at beauty. What further analysis do you need?"

—Sir Elton John

"I think it was fitting that Elton John altered 'Candle in the Wind' after Princess Diana died. It's still well-known he wrote it about Marilyn Monroe, and now it's still about a pretty but insecure girl who became a beautiful and good-hearted but not quite confident enough woman and victim."   —Colin Farrell

"It's startlingly impressive that, since her death, Marilyn Monroe has remained such a sex symbol. For each and every generation. There's been no diminishing of that, and there's nothing remotely necrophilic about it."
—Michelle Pfeiffer

"Much of a star's legacy depends on what they didn't do. Like not living to seventy or eighty. If they're beautiful and retire at forty, like Brigitte Bardot, then you'll see photos of her growing old, but there won't be the embarrassing movie roles of, say, Mae West, who played sexy into her eighties.

   "Some stars act until the very end, like Bette Davis, accepting unflattering roles because they're the best of what's offered. Others retire as senior citizens. What would Marilyn Monroe have done? Would she have become a character actress? . . . I think the fair thing is to judge any actor by their best work, and Marilyn's best is as good as anyone else's."   —Katherine Helmond, TV star, *Soap* and *Who's the Boss?*

"With Marilyn, there's so much to her persona and her story and all she stands for, that whatever you choose to say about her reveals as much or more about you, really, than it does about her."   —Kate Beckinsale

"A lot of lesbians identify with Marilyn because she was practically bred to be a victim but overcame that. Even though she died young, in a way that was a triumph for her. Other than for some religious figures, death has done more for her than it has for hardly anybody else."   —k. d. lang, Canadian singer-songwriter

"Weight-challenged women have sympathy for Marilyn. You'd think we might be jealous. We're not. We can see she's lovely and had a great body. Good for her. But she too was a martyr to looksism—the idea that women are valued mostly for how they look."
—Henriette Mantel, comedian

"I used to want to look like Liz Taylor. Till she got fat and started looking like me. So now I'd rather look like Marilyn Monroe. Let's face it, who wants to look like themselves?"
—Divine, drag actor

"Half the time, a young actress wanted to look like Elizabeth Taylor, and half the time like Marilyn Monroe. Both were such icons of beauty, and even if you were pretty you tended to measure yourself against one or the other."
—Natalie Wood

"How often, in the 1960s, I was told to be more like Marilyn Monroe. . . . After she died, the race was on as to who would be the new Marilyn? Nobody had the brains to realize that there couldn't be a new one. Being blonde is the exception, but Marilyn was a unique entity, and none among us wanted to become a pale imitation. But the executives in charge kept hoping one of us would take her place at the box office."   —Stella Stevens

"I was hired by Fox partly as a 'threat' to Marilyn Monroe. So if she misbehaved or went AWOL, they'd wave me at her and she'd come running back. They did use me but let me go after four years. That was a disappointment at the same time that it was a relief. I didn't have to try and be a Marilyn clone anymore."   —Sheree North, actress

"Mamie Van Doren was the made-up name for Joan Olander. She was bleached platinum to try and 'out-Marilyn' Marilyn Monroe. She got some flashy roles but they didn't lead to very much. . . . Mamie was blatant where Marilyn was subtle. Eventually she took her clothes off in a sexploitation comedy I did. But by then nudity wasn't news. Nor even necessarily box office."

—Tommy Noonan, Marilyn's love interest in *Gentlemen Prefer Blondes*

"Jayne Mansfield wanted a slice, preferably large, of Marilyn Monroe's success. She couldn't compete on Marilyn's level, so she slipped into caricature. The mammoth bust she couldn't help, but she flaunted it day and night . . . overacted the dumb blonde way too often. Took on the tackiest assignments. And then died that unexpected grizzly death in a car accident. It was a tragic ending to a pathetic career."

—Ray Danton, Mansfield's costar in *The George Raft Story*

"Whereas there's a bevy of famous photos of Marilyn, there's just one of Jayne Mansfield, and its subject isn't really Jayne, it's her melon-like, almost-exposed mammaries. Next to Jayne is Sophia Loren, staring down in amazement at that rather ludicrous bust. Now, Loren herself was well endowed, but not so overly and she wasn't an exhibitionist. That photo perfectly illustrates the comedy-skit nature of Miss Mansfield's persona and desperation."   —Eileen Heckart, costar, *Bus Stop*

"Classical statues of goddesses had blank eyes, no irises, allowing the spectator to fill in the quality or emotion. Depending on the eyebrows and expression, if there was one, the goddess seems to challenge or invite the spectator. When studio portraits of movie actresses began, in the silent era, a star was sometimes told to study those ancient sculptures.

"Marilyn Monroe obviously studied faces, particularly her own in a mirror. In ever so many of her posed shots, her half-lidded eyes both challenge and invite the spectator."

—Frank Powolny, studio photographer

"Most analyses of the Monroe face focus on the beautiful lips. But for me it was the eyes that did the trick. That promised so much. Part of her appeal was she seemed able to give more than she could take, and she liked to pose for photographs with her eyes half closed. As if already in ecstasy."
—Fernando Lamas, Argentine actor and heartthrob

"Marilyn had lucky eyelids. She didn't require lots of eye makeup, which studies say is off-putting to most men. All she had to do was half shut her eyes as if her head were on a pillow, and she had these wonderful lids that reached up to her just-so eyebrows, which were never too artificially thin."   —Kevyn Aucoin, makeup artist

"I think Marilyn had the most alluring eyes ever. If you look at just the bottom half of her face, it might be one of several beautiful actresses. But if you look only at the upper half, that can only be Marilyn Monroe."   —Charlie Earle, movie publicist

"It's almost disconcerting that in her movies Marilyn's eyes were most often ingenuous. Very straightforward. By contrast, in her stills she uses her eyes as sensual magnets."

—Marie Windsor, actress, *The Narrow Margin*

"When Marilyn's character looks at an actor in a scene, she often has a beseeching quality in her eyes. It's like she's needy, but she's been hurt before and doesn't want to be hurt again, so she's wondering if she can really depend on this guy."

—Penny Singleton, star of twenty-eight movies based on the *Blondie* comic strip

"Don't hate me for saying this, but if Marilyn Monroe had lived, it would have absolutely killed me to see her playing a grandmother. Do you know what I mean?"

—Hugh Grant

"Sex symbols' headshots are typically eye candy. But Marilyn Monroe invested hers with a combination of seduction and otherworldliness. You look and admire . . . yet in a way it's like looking at a classical work of art in a museum. Andy Warhol caught that when he did his famous portrait of Marilyn. She's a woman, but she's also art."   —Timothy Hutton

"Sadly, it's unsurprising how very seldom Marilyn Monroe was described as a woman in her own time. The descriptions 'girl' and 'child-woman' were applied far more often. It was a way of keeping her in her place, or trying to. The patriarchy she lived under feared questioning, self-motivating women. . . . A child is dependent on an adult, and the whole idea was to keep women at the 'girl' stage, therefore dependent on adults, meaning men."

—Jane Fonda

"Marilyn was a smart cookie and, when she had to be, a tough one. But she wasn't hardened. She kept a childlike quality that was endearing. It was a big asset to her as a performer. It was a liability to her as a trusting adult who was often disappointed and betrayed."
–Olympia Dukakis

"Slightly dizzy or dumb blondes were very accepted then. It was part of the culture, especially in the States. People condescended to that, but they didn't ostracize—it was entertainment. A dumb brunette might have been ostracized. . . . I couldn't have played the roles Marilyn Monroe did. Luckily, being English, it was automatically assumed I was smart."
–Joan Collins

"Lauren Bacall was very sexy despite or because of her low voice. When they costarred in *How to Marry a Millionaire*, they got along very well—as they did with Betty Grable. Marilyn was very admiring of Bacall, including her voice. She thought maybe Bacall was taken more seriously because of it. In the film, Lauren, who's Jewish, is the smart one; Marilyn and Betty are the blonde followers.

"Also, Marilyn thought Bacall's sex appeal derived from being so confident. Marilyn mistakenly thought her own sex appeal came from her face and figure, in toto. She hadn't confidence enough to realize that her entire package was sexy, that the makeup and hair were just frosting on the cake."
–Jean Negulesco, director, *How to Marry a Millionaire*

"A mutual friend said Marilyn once read an article that said if a woman raised her voice too often it would deepen or become gravelly and men would shun her. Obviously the poor soul wanted anything but that. Who knows if that's why she spoke the way she did on screen?"

—Eve Arden

"To this day, people watching her movies are fascinated by Marilyn's voice. Many imitate it, for fun. But if you watch several of her films you'll hear that it wasn't always the same. She did, though, tend to go back to the famous baby voice because, well, it got her the most pats on the head."

—Anne Bancroft

"One impression you get when you look at photos of Marilyn Monroe is she was probably someone who got along with everyone. You don't look at her and think, oh, she probably never threw a tantrum or threw her weight around. That's nonrealistic, but it's a popular ideal and one that sells."
—Catherine Zeta-Jones

"Marilyn could stand up for herself, but not that often . . . not that well. Compared to a Stanwyck, a Susan Hayward, or Elizabeth Taylor, she was putty. So the powers that be walked all over her any chance they got. Too often she let them get away with it."

—Henry Hathaway, director, *Niagara*

"Some people will look at or watch Marilyn and come away with the rather masochistic quality that she had. Others will emphasize her positive qualities and her strength."

—Kathy Bates

"Marilyn Monroe embodies the contradictions of her era and the budding sexual liberation of the '60s with the freedom and modern attitudes of today."
—Harry Belafonte

"How much foresight did Miss Monroe possess? It's extraordinary that in 1949, as a working actress, she posed nude for [Tom Kelley] knowing that every Hollywood studio contract included a morals clause. If one contravened it, one could be instantly fired. Nudity was a prime taboo, as were homosexual and interracial relationships . . . an entire catalogue of offences."
—Anthony Steel, British actor

"Marilyn Monroe, working so hard to become famous, had to be aware that, once famous, her nude calendar photos would surface. She took a tremendous risk. It seems self-destructive, unless she fervently believed that when the moment of revelation came—and how could it not?—she would reap major publicity and be able to ride out the storm."
—Ross Hunter, film and TV producer

"What Marilyn represents, primarily, is beauty. She's the poster girl for beauty. The fact that she died young means there are no ugly photos. We can stare, admire, ogle—and it's free."
—Beatrice Arthur

"I hate those people who say dying young was a wonderful career move on the part of Marilyn and James Dean, et cetera. To me, that's the definition of cynicism. Did Marilyn or Jimmy Dean have a choice? Sure, they may have flirted with death on occasion, but I doubt either was intentionally aiming at an early death, let alone doing it for the publicity."
—Dale Olson, publicist

"James Dean and Marilyn Monroe are often linked together since their deaths. They represent endless youth. I doubt they ever met, but they symbolize young people who went their own way but couldn't defeat the system. I think that's why they're held in awe and pitied—the system eventually did them in."

—Milton Berle, who did a cameo in Marilyn's *Let's Make Love*

"James Dean died in his early twenties, Marilyn in her mid-thirties. I don't sec much connection. He was surly and self-destructive. She was needful and tortured. His career was barely starting, hers was veering toward its end. He was so-so looking, she was still ravishing. The cult around people who die young isn't the healthiest, but it's legitimized by religious figures who died young."

—Rex Reed, film critic

"Like practically everyone else, I was a fan of the lady. Since she died, I've had a pleasant shock or two, seeing my name in the same sentence with Marilyn Monroe's. Of course that's only till I catch on that they're talking about another Jimmy Dean, the actor properly named James Dean."

—Jimmy Dean, entertainer and entrepreneur

"Had Jimmy Dean lived, he'd have had a long and probably varied career ahead of him unless he chose to come out of the closet, which he was hinting at. But Marilyn, as an actress and one very reliant on her appearance, could have been washed up by forty-five or so. Who can say what would have become of her as an actress had she lived?"

—Dawn Steel, former Columbia Pictures president

"I was a blonde bombshell, but I walked away from it. Continuing on that fur-lined road to the loony bin would have killed me, like it did Marilyn Monroe. So I wound up poor, so? I survived and I did it on my own terms. Like Edith Piaf said, I regret nothing, buster."   —Veronica Lake, 1940s pinup and Paramount star

"After Marilyn Monroe died, a number of show business insiders thought it would be a big boost for Jayne Mansfield, including Jayne. It didn't work out that way. Jayne survived Marilyn by about five years, nobody replaced Marilyn, and Jayne's descent was sad to watch—and almost nobody watched."
—Tommy Noonan, who worked with both

"In 1980 I was in a TV movie called *Marilyn: The Untold Story*. But everything had already been told, including that I was one of the Monroe clones. I'm seven years younger than she was and now I've survived Marilyn by over forty years. . . . If I ever felt competitive with Marilyn, today I feel nothing but compassion for her. I wish she were still alive. Alive and happy."   —Sheree North, actress

"Movie stardom looks fabulous from the outside. It can bring good things, marvelous things . . . but it doesn't erase bad ones. The lingering pain inflicted by an uncaring parent is permanent. Marilyn Monroe knew this and I know this. . . . At any rate, I didn't try to erase my pain with drugs. Sooner or later they take their toll, as Marilyn tragically found out."

—Kim Novak (born Marilyn Novak and also seven years Marilyn Monroe's junior)

"Frank Sinatra was a bad influence on her. Not only because he could be an abusive lover, but the hoodlums and rough characters surrounding him. . . . Frank could treat a woman like a duchess for several minutes, then go all iceberg or worse without provocation. He bored easily. . . . During her final year, Marilyn was being led astray by Frank. He took pride in introducing her to his friends and then leaving her alone with them."
—Cameron Mitchell, costar, *How to Marry a Millionaire*

"As celebrities and Italian Americans, DiMaggio and Sinatra had been friends. The exact nature of their rupture isn't clear, but to some extent it involved Marilyn Monroe."
—Anthony Franciosa, actor

"It was Hollywood that destroyed her—she was the victim of her friends."
—Joe DiMaggio, ex-husband

"I feel bad about all the wonderful film performances Marilyn could
have given us had she lived and that we could still be enjoying.
She made too few films and too many mistakes."
—Dorothy Manners, columnist

"The only big movie star sex symbol that followed Marilyn Monroe was Raquel Welch. The public didn't want another blonde, I think out of respect for Marilyn. Maybe also because so many blonde actresses died young. Raquel was tough. Tough, gorgeous, and minimum personality. Men desired after her and women didn't like her. Women liked Marilyn. She was America's last great sex symbol. But you know, in the end it wasn't even about sex. It was about *her*."
—Roy Scheider, actor, *Jaws*

"Most sex symbols are just faces in photos or women in movies. Two hours of entertainment, and that's that. Seldom an emotional connection. Sure, if it's someone like Rita Hayworth, who got Alzheimer's fairly early, you feel sorry for her. But with Marilyn there's a stronger connection."
                                                                                    —Hugh Jackman

"Marilyn Monroe wasn't an actual orphan, but she gave off that vibe. Sometimes you wanted to be her father or mother."
                                                                                    —Bob Hope

"I believe people feel more protective about her than any other star. Men and women. Young and old, and mostly people who weren't even alive when she was."   —John Travolta

"Marilyn is like a relative. She'd literally be as old as your grandmother is today, but she's forever young and she's the sister you wanted to take care of."
                                                                        —Isaac Mizrahi, fashion designer

"There's a proprietary feeling about Marilyn Monroe.
If you heard a criticism, you'd want to defend her.
'Shut up, she's perfect!' And not just because she's dead."
—Peter Fonda

"The key to her endless popularity in visual media is that Marilyn did so many photographic sessions. She loved it, did it often, did it beautifully and imaginatively. So there's a superabundance of pictures of her that you see in shop windows and posters, et cetera, all over the world."
                                                                        —Richard Avedon, photographer

"I was walking in Istanbul. I passed a beauty parlor. It had photos of several local women and a bigger one of Marilyn Monroe. I smiled. Later that day, at a souvenir shop for tourists, two posters of Marilyn. Not for sale—just decoration. Just happying-up the premises."
                                                    —Jules Dassin, director, *Topkapi*

"In many countries, away from the reach of her estate and its licensing and lawyers, you'll find images of Marilyn Monroe being used to advertise you name it. The most impressive thing is that after all this time, she still draws."
—George Clooney

"Other than one reform-minded rabbi about two thousand years ago, I don't think anyone else's early death has resulted in so much veneration."   —Bela Lugosi Jr., attorney

"To die at the top of one's game is to not have been forced to share with the public your descent down the ladder that you once climbed and reached the top of. Obviously it's too bad she died at thirty-six, but if Marilyn Monroe had died at forty-six or fifty-six, would she be remembered as affectionately? You know how most people are."
                                                    —Mary Wickes, character actress

"Marilyn didn't live to need a face-lift and only had very minor plastic surgery when she was starting out. . . . With dieting and plastic surgery, one can look good for a long time— look at Sophia Loren in her seventies. Unlike Brigitte Bardot, who's the same age, but everything sags. I'll bet Marilyn would still have looked good."
                                                    —Max Showalter, costar, *Niagara*

"Marilyn would have been eighty this year [2006]. . . . That's very difficult to picture. In fact impossible. But you needn't think of an old crone. In her eighties Mae West made her last movie, as a woman who is irresistible to men. Some stars are capable of anything. That's why they're stars."   —Cyd Charisse, costar, *Something's Got to Give*

"They don't guess or computer-image how Marilyn Monroe would have looked like today. People don't want to tamper with perfection."   —Paul Winfield, actor, *Sounder*

"Marilyn would be ninety years old next year [2016]. . . . More and more people, especially women, are living into their nineties. Doris Day's still alive, two years older than Marilyn. . . . Still, Marilyn at ninety—somehow it doesn't fit. Because Marilyn's still young. Forever young. Forever Marilyn."
—Neil Patrick Harris

"Not long before she died, she lost eighteen pounds. She'd been taken aback by her swimsuit scene in *The Misfits*. So for *Something's Got to Give*, Marilyn dieted back to [a] fantastic shape and looks. Many of us were pleasantly surprised that she had the discipline and the motivation. Then everything came crashing down on her."
—Irving Rapper, director (who lived to 101)

"Toward the end, Marilyn's hair went from blonde to platinum. Instead of looking phony, it made her look ethereal. More like a heavenly being than a Hollywood star. So we have those fabulous visuals of her to crown the legend."   —George Masters, hairdresser

"I daresay Marilyn Monroe still makes more people smile than any other dead celebrity."

—Dame Maggie Smith

"With all the retakes and all her late arrivals on the set, there was often grumbling and even threats about forcibly retiring Marilyn Monroe. But they didn't. Not only she made them money, she made magic."   —Elliott Reid, costar, *Gentlemen Prefer Blondes*

"Millions of people have seen Marilyn Monroe's motion pictures. But billions have seen her *pictures*."   —Salma Hayek, actress, *Frida*

"I have reversed my position. Marilyn Monroe was a talented cinematic presence. From what I've heard of her time in New York studying 'the Method' she was apparently effective on stage, as well. More's the pity that she didn't pursue acting on the stage. It would have given her more satisfaction and prestige than any imaginable motion picture."

—Sir Laurence Olivier

"At least by thirty she should have chosen to be in a play. She'd have been a sellout. Who wouldn't go see her perform, and even if the critics had been expectedly unkind, her courage would have been admired."
—Rose Marie, actress, *The Dick Van Dyke Show*

"The roles Monroe was doing into her thirties were almost identical to the ones she'd done a decade before. Not much variation or evolution. But whose fault, really? Producers only saw her one way."   —James Card, film preservationist

"Marilyn Monroe is pure cinema. . . . Watch her work in any film. How rarely she has to use words. How much she does with her eyes, her lips, with slight, almost accidental gestures."

—Joshua Logan, director, *Bus Stop*

"Once sound came in, movie voices became almost as important as faces. . . . Marilyn Monroe's speaking voice has sometimes been ridiculed. But close your eyes and just listen—it's very reassuring, a pleasant voice. This was brought home to me when I saw some of her films on television in Europe and she was dubbed into different languages. It always sounded wrong, sometimes dreadful—a monotone or a grating voice that had nothing to do with the actress who was no longer saying the lines."

—Viveca Lindfors, Swedish actress, *The Way We Were*

"Was Marilyn Monroe a good actress? The same was asked of Greta Garbo, the leading female star of the first half of the twentieth century. It's an irrelevant question. What matters, still, is that each was a wonderful actress."
—Ed Asner

"Marilyn Monroe had lousy luck to blossom during a mixed-up, hypocritical part of our history. Remember the very low-cut gold gown she wore to that awards show that was designed for *Gentlemen Prefer Blondes* but hardly seen in the movie? Marilyn posed in it for a from-the-waist-up photo, in full sex-goddess mode. The picture was widely distributed, however, her cleavage was airbrushed out!

"So the figure was sexy yet sexless. There was still sexiness, though—on Marilyn's face. They couldn't airbrush that."

—Sue Mengers, superstar agent

"Marilyn is a bountiful icon because she expresses both sides of the American political cultural coin—the rich possibilities and costs of dreaming an American life."

—S. Paige Baty, sociologist

"I miss her. It was like going to the dentist, making a picture with her. It was hell at the time, but after it was over, it was wonderful." —Earl Wilson, Hollywood columnist

"Marilyn Monroe, who was blonde and beautiful and had a sweet little rinky-dink of a voice and all the cleanliness of all the clean American backyards. She was our angel."
—Norman Mailer, novelist and MM biographer

"Marilyn had a childlike quality which made men adore her. Yet women weren't jealous."

—Ben Lyon, Fox talent director

"I remember how Jane Fonda's popularity plummeted when she, a sexy girl next door, opened her mouth and expressed opinions about an unjust war and discrimination against minorities in America. At once and literally she was on an 'enemies list.'" —Jack Lemmon

"The female public's envy of Marilyn Monroe was tempered by the disadvantages she'd had and the assorted lows in Marilyn's life. With beautiful, sensual stars who never seemed to suffer or who married princes and zillionaires, women fans had less patience."

—Harry Brand, Fox publicity executive

"I saw ordinary everyday women, young or middle-aged, who were as thrilled to have their picture taken with Marilyn Monroe as they would have been with any of the top leading men. Marilyn was equal-opportunity excitement. She wove a spell."

—Earl Leaf, photojournalist

"Marilyn Monroe was a forbidden delight of the 1950s. Had she lived in the Middle Ages and looked the way she did, she'd have been burned at the stake. Patriarchal men tend to dislike and fear that which turns them on. The ability to turn someone on implies a certain power over them, however fleeting."
—Barbara Tuchman, historian

"At her peak, Marilyn received ten thousand fan letters a week, more than any other star. Most weren't mash notes or love letters, but letters from the heart, from both genders—probably even more from females—to someone special who seemed lovable yet accessible, somebody worth writing to. There was a powerful connection there."
—Sybil Brand, Los Angeles philanthropist and wife of Fox publicity chief Harry Brand

"I knew her more as a peer and escort [to public functions] than as a friend. I liked her. She was funny and endearing. . . . If ever a woman was sexy, she was. But more importantly, Marilyn was friendly."

—Rock Hudson

"Ah, I liked her so much. She was a nice lady. So witty."

—Saul Bellow, Pulitzer Prize–winning novelist

"She was the type who would join in and wash up the supper dishes even if you didn't ask her."

—Carl Sandburg, poet

"The humor! Why do people keep forgetting her sense of humor? She loved to laugh. Okay, she's not laughing now. But while she was alive, if you were in a room with her, sooner or later, usually sooner, there'd be laughter. I can still hear it."

—Tony Randall, costar, *Let's Make Love*

"She communicated such a charge of vitality as altered our imagination of life."

—Diana Trilling, literary and social critic

"Being with her, people want not to die."

—Arthur Miller

"Photos and posters of Marilyn Monroe are more vivid and relevant than [those] of most past sex symbols. My interpretation is it's because of her attitude. She wasn't ashamed. Most who posed weren't, but Marilyn didn't hold back. Most of the others did. Like they were somewhat secretly guilty. Or somewhat selfish."

—Jennifer Lawrence

"She was very natural in front of the camera . . . spontaneous. Even when she seemed distracted, she wasn't unaware of the camera. I've seen early photographs of her sitting in a group with other Hollywood starlets and in some she's the only person looking at the camera. With a little smile playing at the edge of her lips."

—Richard Wattis, costar, *The Prince and the Showgirl*

"The camera almost never caught Marilyn off guard. After a certain point, she knew it was part and parcel of her life. You don't see photos of her looking shocked or surprised by the camera. . . . Even in moments of raw grief, her face didn't look distorted, the way a face does during pain or weeping. When she was sad or heartbroken, as after a miscarriage, or crying, she still did it prettily. The proof is in her photos."

—Kenn Duncan, photographer

"The first sex symbol was Theda Bara, known as the Vamp. Then there were Jean Harlow and Jane Russell and Rita and Lana and Ava, Brigitte and Raquel and Farrah, et cetera. All sexy. Likable? Posed for a photographer, most have a look-but-don't-touch vibe, or else they seem to be sneering, almost daring you. Not myself, but more than a handful of men find that vibe withering."   —William Castle, producer (*Rosemary's Baby*) and director

"Of course I think Marilyn Monroe was sexy. What a dumb question!"
—Madonna

"Before Marilyn, there was one upbeat sex symbol—Betty Grable, a smiling blonde famous for her legs. She did musicals at Fox, where she was a goldmine for them throughout the '40s. In 1953 Fox costarred her with Marilyn Monroe in *How to Marry a Millionaire*. The studio was planning to get rid of her—after all, she was thirty-seven years old. Marilyn, a brand-new star and ten years younger than Grable, was scared that Fox had in mind to do the same to her!"   —Durward Kirby, *Candid Camera* cohost

"She had this absolutely unerring touch with comedy."
—George Cukor, MM's two-time director (*Let's Make Love* and *Something's Got to Give*)

"The greatest thing about Monroe is not her chest. It is her ear. She can read comedy better than anyone else in the world."

    —Billy Wilder, MM's two-time director (*Some Like It Hot* and *The Seven Year Itch*)

"If she was so dumb, how did she go so high and stay so high?
Marilyn knew what worked for her. She knew the business thoroughly."
—Florence Henderson, actress, *The Brady Bunch*

"I've read that some publicists were horrified when she would scissor rejected negatives of photos of herself that she didn't like into little pieces. The usual practice was to draw an X over a negative with a red grease pencil. Marilyn was the expert on how she should look. . . . It goes without saying, or should, that as she grew older, she had to be more careful about which photos would go out to the public.

    "Some people were just waiting for telltale signs of age on her. How Marilyn looked related directly to how hirable she was in the industry."   —Charlie Earle, movie publicist

"Streisand is known to be very picky about her publicity photos. Nowadays most stars, including men, pore over their negatives and select and reject. At the time Marilyn Monroe was doing it, a lot of the stars left it up to their studio. Some women bothered, but most of the men didn't even look.

    "Men stars don't have to be as concerned. . . . They don't have hairstyles and pieces, stray hairs, eyeliner and running mascara or smudged lipstick to deal with. And their popularity isn't as intimately bound up with their appearance."

    —John Kobal, photo archivist

"It wasn't so outrageous that Marilyn destroyed the negatives by cutting them into tiny pieces. . . . With Marilyn, any scrap of her was valuable and would eventually be exploited. No one understood that better than Marilyn. Look what happened after she scratched out the photos she disliked taken by Bert Stern on the negatives. Soon after she died, he released them—all scratched and crossed out! And years after that, they were digitally retouched so that her mark of disapproval was erased forever."

—Charles Casillo, author, *The Marilyn Diaries: A Novel*

"Sheree North told me that when she was at Twentieth Century Fox one day, she ran into Allan 'Whitey' Snyder, who was pacing outside a closed door, very frustrated. She asked him what was wrong. He said, 'Marilyn is in there and she won't let me in. She's making up her own face.'

"I'm not saying Whitey never made up her face. Of course he did. But there were times when all he needed to do was make a touch-up. She, Marilyn, was the real master of that Look."

—James Haspiel, MM biographer

"Miss Monroe is one of the greatest comedy actresses of our time. She is simply superb."

—Vladimir Nabokov, novelist, *Lolita*

"On the Twentieth lot Marilyn came up to me. She was wearing a pair of pedal pushers and flat shoes and a scarf and nobody paid her the slightest bit of attention because she looked like she was fourteen! She went to her dressing room and said, 'Well, time to put her together.' She went into her dressing room and about forty minutes later . . . Marilyn Monroe walked out. It was just a total transformation."

—Michael Shaw, acting coach, who was twenty-two at the time

"Marilyn had makeup tricks that nobody else had and nobody knows."
                                        —Allan "Whitey" Snyder, her makeup man

"We felt so honored that Whitey was our makeup man on *Little House on the Prairie.*'
He had actually touched and made up the face of Marilyn Monroe. Of course we were all
bursting with questions, but if he didn't volunteer something, we didn't have the nerve or
bad taste to ask. He was still broken up about her death."
                                        —Alison Arngrim (aka Nellie Oleson)

"Marilyn needed me like a dead man needs a coffin."
                    —Natasha Lytess, acting coach

"Miss [Eva] Gabor had a heart of Hungarian stone. When Judy Garland died, it was in her
will that she wanted her favorite hairdresser to do her hair for the internment. That there
hairdresser was now working for Eva on our show [*Green Acres*]. But Eva refused to let
her have the day off to go and take care of the late Miss Garland. I'm not one to ever cry or
bawl, but I did shed a private tear for two sad ladies who died way too young, and that was
Marilyn Monroe and Judy Garland."   —Pat Buttram (aka Mr. Haney)

"There may be an exact psychiatric term for what was wrong with her. I don't know . . . I
think she was quite mad. The mother was mad and poor Marilyn was mad."
  —George Cukor, MM's two-time director (*Let's Make Love* and *Something's Got to Give*)

"Our series [*The Patty Duke Show*, in which he played the father] was coproduced by Peter Lawford's company. We were never supposed to ask him anything about Marilyn Monroe and, of course, wouldn't think of doing so. . . . As for the Kennedy rumors, they were barely whispered about.

"But a few friends of Lawford did let slip that Marilyn's friends were worried about her mental health during those last months. Some thought she was becoming paranoid because she would go to pay telephones to make phone calls . . . and some thought she feared for her life. So little of the whole situation was known then . . . not that much is known now."

— William Schallert, later president of the Screen Actors Guild (as was Patty Duke)

"In 1977 a workman repairing the roof of Marilyn Monroe's last residence put his foot through rotted tiles and found the rusted remains of wiring and transmitters, estimated to be fifteen to twenty years old. Were they J. Edgar Hoover's? Sam Giancana's? Jimmy Hoffa's? All three? They all hated the Kennedys, and there has been reason to suspect their collusion on other issues, so why not this? For that matter, were the Kennedys taping her?"
— Michael Ventura, MM biographer

"It's like in the movies, where a woman knows something the others don't, so everyone thinks she's delusional, but she's not, and later some tragedy occurs and she's proven right. Marilyn knew that she was being spied on. Deplorably, what made her less believed is that she was increasingly under the influence of drugs . . . whether that was voluntary or she was being chemically manipulated we can never be certain."

— Dalton Trumbo, blacklisted screenwriter

"She was more nervous than any other actress I have ever known. But nervousness for an actress is not a handicap. It is a sign of sensitivity."

—Lee Strasberg

"Marilyn had always been nervous about her work. She did overcome much of that and gained confidence about acting. She was still nervous about dancing, when she did *Let's Make Love*, so I was brought in as choreographer. By that time Marilyn was less nervous about work matters in general. But she was more nervous about her private life."

—Jack Cole

"In a way we are all guilty. We built her to the skies. We loved her but left her lonely and afraid when she needed us most."
—Hedda Hopper, gossip columnist

"I'm sorry she made the decision she did, sorrier today when I know how it all ended."

—first husband James Dougherty on their divorce

"Stars like Ginger Rogers and Lauren Bacall had mothers to encourage their ambitions, praise their beauty and talents, and give behind-the-scenes support to their careers. Norma Jean was alone. Through the horrors of the '30s Depression, girls her age endured poverty in the bosom of tightly knit families. Norma Jean had no immediate family to count on for the goodnight kiss or morning hug. She had to face the terrors of childhood by herself in the only way she could, through fantasy and the single-minded rage to *be* somebody."

—Jeannie Sakol, writer and journalist

"Marilyn would have been sixty this year [1986].
If the feminist movement had existed, it might have saved her life."
–Gloria Steinem

"Still she hangs like a bat in the heads of men who have met her, and none of us will ever forget her."
                                                                                    –Sammy Davis Jr.

"I salute Marilyn for a major—and unacknowledged—feminist act. Sexually abused as a child, she named that abuse as an adult. She refused to keep quiet in an age that believed such abuse rarely happened, and when it did, the victimized girl was responsible. Such self-disclosure would become important to the feminist movement in the 1970s.

"Neither Ruth Benedict nor Margaret Mead, eminent American anthropologists and public intellectuals whose lives I chronicled, disclosed the episodes of sexual abuse in their childhoods. I didn't expect to find such episodes in any of these lives, but the rates of such abuse have been high throughout our history.

"In an act of great bravery, Marilyn named the abuse she endured."
                                –Lois Banner, USC history professor and author of two books about MM

"She was a fool to kill herself . . . she could have been the first great woman director because she understood how to make movies."
                                                        –Andy Warhol, wrong on both counts
                                (The first great female director was Dorothy Arzner, 1900–1979.)

"Can you think of anyone else who finally became a star and then, instead of profitably coasting on her looks and stardom, decided to become a real actor, took time off from making movies and money, moved away and went to school to learn to act, with her classmates and the press and the whole world watching? That requires singular guts and integrity."
—Robert LaGuardia, author

"In death, as in life, the woman who was Marilyn Monroe continues to exert a power I've never been able to fully understand or explain."   —Ted Jordan, friend and actor

"She was, if I recall correctly, about five feet, five inches, but she seemed smaller. Her childlike voice . . . I wondered to myself if she would register in the film—will she come over? Additionally, acting opposite Larry Olivier. . . . My goodness, she certainly came over!"   —Dame Sybil Thorndike, costar, *The Prince and the Showgirl*

"She was a good talker. She spoke well on the national scene, the Hollywood scene, and on people who are good to know and people who ain't."   —Carl Sandburg, poet

"Marilyn didn't talk about her ex-husbands or boyfriends for public consumption. It must have been part of her code. The first husband probably didn't abuse her, unlike the two famous ones in their differing ways. The one we know hit her was number two. But Marilyn never spilled the beans or said anything critical about any of them."

—Jadin Wong, talent agent

"She pursued an impossible dream. Marilyn Monroe very much wanted to be taken seriously, but she also loved and perpetuated the way she looked and dressed. Even today the two do not go together."   —Jane Curtin, actress-comedian, *Saturday Night Live*

"How often in her lifetime she was taken as a joke. A dirty joke, even. Now there are college courses about Marilyn Monroe. If only she could know and savour it."
—Peter Conradi, British actor and author

"I think if she could come back and see and read everything about her, Marilyn would be horrified and astounded and delighted. The thing she'd definitely like the best would be the reappraisal of her talent."   —Misty Rowe, actress who played MM in a TV movie

"Marilyn played the best game with the worst hand of anybody I know."
—Edward Wagenknecht, author

"One of her worst experiences was the miscarriage of her and Arthur Miller's child. That could have been her last chance for the family life she'd long been seeking. Marilyn died on the anniversary of that miscarriage."   —Barbara Leaming, MM biographer

"Make of it what you will, but Marilyn Monroe and Jacqueline Kennedy both had whispery little-girl voices."
—Cameron Mitchell, costar, *How to Marry a Millionaire*

"I think the shrink and the housekeeper, Dr. Greenson and Mrs. Murray, were plants. Part of whatever cover-up or plot against or around Marilyn Monroe. . . . The elusive truth—is it simpler than we imagine or far more complex?"

—George Peppard, actor, *Breakfast at Tiffany's*

"There's the nagging question of how she could have swallowed so many pills without water on that fatal night."
—James Bacon, Hollywood columnist

"I know that hours before she died, Marilyn telephoned her friend Norman Rosten in New York. She was going to visit him and his family on a trip back east in September and she was really looking forward to it. This was just *hours* before."

—Dr. Michael M. Gurdin, friend

"Robert Kennedy was a different kettle of fish than brother Jack. . . . Equally ambitious, more ruthless . . . let us not forget that initially he toiled for McCarthy the uber-Republican before cleaving to the Democratic fold of his family.

"Don't ask me about the Marilyn and 'Bobby' mess. Ask Robert's friend John Bates. Mr. Bates was with him when our attorney general officially received the news of Marilyn Monroe's death. I don't know how surprised he was or wasn't, but Bates is quoted saying the younger Kennedy took the news 'rather lightly' and they talked about it 'in sort of an amusing way.'"

—Gore Vidal, who sued Truman Capote for saying RFK had ejected him bodily from the White House

"What I'd like to know is, if he had nothing to hide, why did Robert F. Kennedy deny seeing Marilyn Monroe on the last day of her life? He was in California and had a helicopter. . . . Separate sources locate him in Los Angeles on that day, despite his denials. What's behind that? Does that hold the solution to the whole thing?"
—Frankie Vaughan, costar, *Let's Make Love*

"Sad, truly, that she died on a Saturday night, the traditional date night when the young and the restless and attractive are out socializing and enjoying themselves. Marilyn Monroe was America's dream date, yet she was dateless and alone on that final night of her life."
—Billy Crystal

"I've read how Marilyn was all alone on that ultimate day of her life. Not. She had different visitors and also phone callers and her dog Maf. Naturally she was alone in the wee hours, after everyone left. Duh."
—Jennifer Tilly, actress

"I can't help thinking how wrong the public is about movie-star lives, about the imagined fun, glamour, and elegant company we keep. I know what loneliness is. . . . I once was driven to phone Joan Crawford, no less, to invite her out, thinking while I dialed how foolish and presumptuous I was. I almost hung up before she answered, but Miss Crawford was surprised and delighted to be asked out.

"Think how much more nerve it would have taken to call and ask Marilyn Monroe out—and I dearly wish I had."
—Rod Steiger

"No one's ever said that Marilyn was terrified of old age or joked—and many actresses semi-joke about it—that she'd sooner die than be middle-aged or . . . sixty. She didn't like getting older, but I hope it wasn't a major anxiety. She had enough problems."

—Elle MacPherson, model turned actress

"At least she was spared the indignities of age. Those are bad enough for anyone, but worse for somebody beautiful, and worst for a beautiful movie star."

—Dr. Michael M. Gurdin, MM's one-time plastic surgeon

"I suppose for someone as sensitive as Marilyn Monroe, the physical and professional costs of growing older and then old in such a public profession would have practically killed her."

—Joan Collins

"There'll never be anyone like her, for looks, for attitude, for all of it."
—Betty Grable, costar, *How to Marry a Millionaire*

"It's the lips and the eyes, also the hair, but even more importantly it's what's behind them. She's simply the standard portrait of how maximum beautiful a human being can look."

—Jackie Collins

"That thing about her eyes . . . half-shut, like she's here but half in a dream world. When they were wide open, which wasn't often, it was a more inquiring or surprised look. Marilyn did wonderful things with her eyes—things many of us have tried to duplicate but can't. It must have been built in."

—Sharon Gless, actress, *Cagney and Lacey*

143

"Marilyn Monroe is all things to all people. She can symbolize almost anything you want."
—Dr. Joyce Brothers, psychologist

"You know how in the old days so many actresses went to a premiere or event wearing a corsage or holding a big flower or small bouquet? Maybe that was considered feminine, but it distracted from their face. Marilyn Monroe didn't have to do that. She was her own flower."
—Neil Patrick Harris

"Marilyn was all things to all people."
—Madonna

"She was and is the eternal feminine."
—Omar Sharif

"Marilyn Monroe is the symbol par excellence of the American girl."
—Gérard Depardieu, French star

"Marilyn was the best homegrown product Hollywood ever produced. Then proceeded to milk dry until nothing was left."
—Ralph Roberts, masseur and friend

"When she was alive she might represent unfulfillment. Now she's dead she represents beauty and optimism. She's typically smiling."
—Johnny Depp

"Hers and the Mona Lisa's have to be the most famous and analyzed smiles of all."
—Helena Bonham Carter

"No one is young forever unless they die young, beautiful, and famous. It's a wonderful dream. If you're alive to dream it." —Stella Adler, acting coach

"Marilyn Monroe was like a dream of Marilyn Monroe." —Lee Strasberg

"To pass away before middle age is to retain and achieve eternal youth. The writer Yukio Mishima believed in the cult of the body beautiful and planned his premature death. Without planning, it worked better for Marilyn Monroe than anyone in the history of Hollywood." —Toshiro Mifune, Japanese actor

"No other star can touch Marilyn Monroe's posthumous success. Or ever will." —Cher

"She will go on eternally."
—Jacqueline Kennedy Onassis

"Less than a year before she died, Marilyn Monroe bought her first home, on Fifth Helena Drive in the Brentwood area of Los Angeles. Below its front door a four-part engraved tile in Latin read *Cursum Perficio*. People preferring the half-empty-glass approach to life translated it as 'My journey ends here,' some of them stating that Marilyn had it put in, intending to die there.

"The tile was part of the house when it was built, some three decades before Marilyn purchased it, and the translation is 'I complete the course.' The motto, found on houses in various European countries, affirms the half-full-glass approach to life."
—Boze Hadleigh, MM historian

Marilyn in Her Own Words

"I dreamed of becoming so beautiful that people would turn and look at me when I passed."

"When I was a little girl I read signed stories in the fan magazines, and I believed every word the stars said in them."

"I guess I've always had too much fantasy to be only a housewife."

"If I'd observed all the rules, I'd never have got anywhere."

"Sometimes I'm invited places to kind of brighten up a dinner table. You're just an ornament."

"I could actually feel my lack of talent, as if it were cheap clothes I was wearing inside. But my God, how I wanted to learn . . . I didn't want anything else. Not men, not money, not love, but the ability to act."

"When you are famous every weakness is exaggerated."

"Being a movie actress was never as much fun as dreaming of being one."

"Hollywood's a place where they'll pay you a thousand dollars for a kiss and fifty cents for your soul."

"I'm not interested in money. I just want to be wonderful."

"I'm so many people. Sometimes I wish I was just me."

"I guess I look for freedom. Freedom from myself, even."

"They think I'm dumb because of the parts I play. If I play a stupid girl and ask a stupid question I've got to follow it through. What am I supposed to do—look intelligent?"

"I think I have one talent: observing. I hope that it adds up to acting."

"When the photographers come, it's like looking in a mirror. They think they arrange me to suit themselves, but I use them to put over myself. It's necessary in the movie business."

"Pretty is just how good you apply your base."

"I've given pure sex appeal very little thought. If I had to think about it I'm sure it would frighten me."

"If I'm going to be a symbol of something I'd rather have it sex than some other things we've got symbols of."

"I'm always running into people's unconscious."

"The truth is I've never fooled anyone. I've let men sometimes fool themselves. Men sometimes didn't bother to find out who and what I was. Instead they would invent a character for me. I wouldn't argue with them. They were obviously loving somebody I wasn't. When they found this out, they would blame me for disillusioning them—and fooling them."

"I like animals. If you talk to a dog or a cat it doesn't tell you to shut up."

"There was a period when I responded too much to flattery. . . . I always liked the guy at the time. They were always so full of self-confidence and I had none at all and they made me feel better."

"I want to be an artist, not an erotic freak. I don't want to be sold to the public as a celluloid [*sic*] aphrodisical—look at me and start shaking. . . . It was all right for the first few years. But now it's different."

"Anything's possible, almost."

"I'm nobody's slave and never have been. Nobody hypnotizes me to do this or that. . . . I didn't get help from my directors. I had to find it elsewhere."

"Some of those bastards in Hollywood wanted me to drop Arthur [Miller], said it would ruin my career. They're born cowards and they want you to be like them."

"Just as I had once fought to get into the movies and become an actress, I would now have to fight to become myself."

"Sometimes people start tailing me. I don't mind. I realize some people want to see if you're real."

"Somehow I feel they know that I mean what I do. I always do mean 'Hello' and 'How are you?'"

"It's often just enough to be with someone. I don't even need to touch them. Not even talk. A feeling passes between you both. You're not alone."

"See if I'm worth being a friend. That's up to you, and you figure it out after a while."

"I want to grow old without face-lifts. . . . I want to have the courage to be loyal to the face I've made."

"You've got to get the most out of the moment."

"It might be a kind of relief to be finished."

"If only they would be honest—just once."

"Fame will go by and, so long, I've had you, fame."

ACKNOWLEDGMENTS

As always, Ronald Boze provided the most help, with the added bonus of clippings galore via Linda Fresia.

I thank my agents Stephen A. Fraser and Jennifer DeChiara, editor Rick Rinehart, editor Ellen Urban, and publicist Jessica Plaskett.

Also Lois Banner, Joshua Barnes, Ken Ferguson, E. J. Fleming, James Ireland Baker, Jim Key, Chad Oberhausen, Ron Sebahar, Cyril Shanahan, Jay Walton, and Gordon Warnock, plus numerous actors, publicists, and others quoted in this collection.

Additionally, any fan would do well to visit, among other quality websites, marilynremembered.com, marilynmonroepages.com, lovingmarilyn.com, and immortalmarilyn.com.

PHOTO CREDITS

ABOUT THE AUTHOR

Boze Hadleigh is the author of twenty-two books, including *An Actor Succeeds*, *Celebrity Feuds!*, and *Broadway Babylon*. His writing has been translated into fourteen languages. He holds a master's degree in journalism, speaks five languages, has visited more than seventy countries, and won on *Jeopardy!*—donating his winnings to a fire-damaged library. Hadleigh divides his time between Beverly Hills, Sydney, and Hong Kong.